Tales from the
Iowa Sidelines

BY RON MALY

Sports Publishing L.L.C.
www.sportspublishingllc.com

Director of production: Susan M. Moyer
Project manager: Tracy Gaudreau
Developmental editor: Erin Linden-Levy
Copy editor: Cynthia L. McNew
Dust jacket design: Kenneth J. O'Brien
Interior photos provided by University of Iowa AV Photo Service

ISBN: 1-58261-574-8

Printed in the United States

Sports Publishing L.L.C.
www.sportspublishingllc.com

TO MY WIFE, MAXINE, who said, "Well, you've probably set the record for writing about Iowa football games, players and coaches over the last 40 years, so go ahead and do it," when I sought her opinion after a guy from Sports Publishing called to ask if I was interested in authoring *Tales from the Iowa Sidelines*. For the next year, she somehow had the patience to put up with me as I researched and wrote these tales.

TO MY SONS AND DAUGHTERS-IN-LAW— Lonn and Julie, Mark and Polly, Kevin and Donna. Now, when they ask me during those Sunday and holiday family dinners how the book is going, I can finally say, "It's finished and it was fun."

AND TO MY SIX WONDERFUL GRANDCHILDREN— Jerika and Shelby, Cole and Claire, Nathan and Megan. Now, when I hear them ask, "Where's Grandpa?" I won't have to holler, "In the computer room, writing about another Iowa football game!"

Contents

When Hayden Fry came north from Texas to coach Iowa in 1979, the school hadn't enjoyed a winning record in 17 seasons. The streak stretched to 19 seasons before Fry coached the Hawkeyes' 1981 team to an 8-4 record that included a trip to the Rose Bowl. Fry was Iowa's coach for 20 years.

Ronald Reagan, who would become the nation's 40th president, was a play-by-play radio broadcaster of Iowa football games in the 1930s. Bill Reichardt, a standout Hawkeye fullback, claims he was the "highest illegally paid player in the history of Iowa football." Then there were Ozzie Simmons, the standout player who hopped a freight train in Texas so he could get to Iowa, and Ossie Solem, his coach.

Acknowledgments

Thanks to Bob Brooks, Ron Gonder, Jim Zabel, Gary Dolphin, Al Grady and George Wine, whose wonderful storytelling abilities helped make the writing of *Tales from the Iowa Sidelines* a pleasure.

Introduction

This book started out to be about football, basketball and wrestling at the University of Iowa.

Then...

Wouldn't you know it? Coach Kirk Ferentz and his 2002 Hawkeye football team won a school-record 11 games, tied for the Big Ten championship with an 8-0 record, and suddenly I suggested to the folks at Sports Publishing, "We've got a winner here. How about saving the basketball and wrestling for the next book?"

They went along with the idea. So here we are with not only the best tales from a 2002 season that turned into something special, but also a rich assortment of anecdotes from other eras in the university's football history.

Iowa put its first team on the field in 1889, and it was not very pretty. There was no coach and no offense. The team was shut out in its only game, 24-0.

But better things would eventually be on the way. Along came Howard Jones, Dr. Eddie Anderson, Forest Evashevski, Hayden Fry and Ferentz, who all coached the Hawkeyes to big games and big seasons. They're all in this book.

And along came the likes of Nile Kinnick, Bill Reichardt, Kenny Ploen, Cal Jones, Alex Karras, Randy Duncan, Bob Stoops, Chuck Long, Chuck Hartlieb, Marv Cook, Larry Station, Tim Dwight, Tavian Banks, Brad Banks and many other players to do the running, passing, receiving, blocking and tackling. They're in the book, too.

When I was 13, I spent a week in the children's section of University Hospital at Iowa City, and a wonderful bunch of nurses worked it out so that I could attend my first Iowa football game at a place that wasn't to be named Kinnick Stadium until 1972. The Hawkeyes defeated Wisconsin 19-13 that day, and I was hooked.

The next year, I sat in the Knothole section for the Northwestern game. Iowa won that day, too, 28-21. Within a few years, I went from kid-in-the-Knothole-section to photographer's spotter on the sideline during Evashevski's outstanding seasons. At the time, I was working as a part-timer at the *Cedar Rapids Gazette* while attending Iowa. Later, from 1965-1998, I thoroughly enjoyed working in stadiums and press boxes around the nation while covering games for the *Des Moines Register.*

Writing about Iowa football was, and always has been, a roller-coaster ride. During one stage, five Hawkeye coaches had 19 consecutive non-winning seasons. Frankly, I was starting to wonder what would come first—the end of the streak or my retirement from the newspaper business. But Fry eventually showed that there could, indeed, be life in the Hawkeye program again. After him came Ferentz and his brilliant coaching job in 2002.

In my estimation, a 38-17 loss to Southern California in the Orange Bowl cost Ferentz's Hawkeyes their chance to become the best team ever at Iowa. Still, it's obvious that Ferentz has brought back the fire and the fun to the Hawkeye program.

Finally, one more personal note. After many interviews with the people in this book, my one regret is that I wasn't old enough to see Kinnick and his 1939 Ironmen play. Kinnick—not big and not fast—was a special player and a special person. He captured the imagination of an entire nation.

In my conversations with those who knew him, played with him and played against him, I am convinced the 5'8", 170-pound Kinnick was destined for greatness beyond the football field. He remains the most dynamic player in the 113-year history of football at the university. At 24, he died much too young in the June 2, 1943 crash of his navy fighter plane.

Chapter 1
The Kirk Ferentz Years

And the New Coach Is...

Nothing lasts forever.

Fans who had watched Hayden Fry turn Iowa's football program from Big Loser to Big Winner in a 20-year period knew he'd retire sometime.

Sometime came following the 1998 season.

The Hawkeyes had only a 3-8 record that year, and Fry was obviously tired.

Sick, too.

Several years after he retired, Fry told me he had "lost all my energy" during his final season. His problem was eventually diagnosed as prostate cancer.

So where would athletic director Bob Bowlsby and other University of Iowa officials look to find Fry's successor?

Bob Stoops's name was a hot one in collegiate coaching circles at the time, and he seemed to be the guy many fans wanted. Stoops had played at Iowa from 1979-82, and a number of his friends thought he'd be the ideal successor to Fry.

Stoops had been a standout assistant coach at Kansas State under Bill Snyder and Florida under Steve Spurrier.

He Seemed Ready for the Iowa Challenge

Bowlsby had obviously heard Stoops's name mentioned many times.

"The talk about Bob Stoops had been around even during the last couple of years Hayden was our coach," Bowlsby said. "That was always the package—'Hayden needs to retire and we need to hire Bob Stoops.'

"Bob had been at a couple of places that were different than Iowa. I think he may have thought, and others may have thought, that this should be a turn-key deal. You go out and tap him on the shoulder and offer him 'X' number of dollars and that's the end of it.

"But it doesn't work that way. We had a number of quality candidates. I talked with Bob over the course of this process. I called him the first day after Hayden's retirement—and he was the first guy I called. Through that process, we set up an interview time."

Someone with Stoops's assistant coaching credentials usually never has just one job opportunity.

"I was aware that he was talking to Oklahoma as well," Bowlsby said. "But I had made a commitment to also interview Kirk Ferentz. Ultimately, it came down to us interviewing Stoops, and Bob saying at the time, 'I have an offer on the table, and I've got to know right now [where I stand with Iowa].'

"I said, 'I've given my word that I would interview Kirk Ferentz and would ask you to wait 24 hours until I've made good on that obligation.'"

The 24-hour wait did not occur.

"Either it had been done already or it was done later that evening that Stoops told Oklahoma he wanted to go ahead and be their coach," Bowlsby said

"I don't blame him. I wasn't able to credibly give him a wink and a nod at that point because I told Kirk he'd have an opportunity to be considered for the job. I felt I needed to stand by that.

"Bob Stoops is a good guy. He's a good coach. He and Kirk Ferentz were good friends when Kirk was Iowa's offensive line coach and Bob was a graduate assistant here. Much has been made of it, but Bob and I see each other at meetings and I don't think there are any hard feelings on my part or his."

Added Bowlsby: "If you took 100 football coaches and put them in a room, 99 of them would take the Oklahoma job over the Iowa job. Even if Bob Stoops had an offer for both jobs, it might have been tough to not take the Oklahoma job."

Stoops Says He Wasn't Offered the Job

Bob Stoops, a four-year letterman at Iowa who later was a graduate assistant and volunteer coach at the school, was Florida's defensive coordinator and assistant head coach when the Hawkeyes were looking for the successor to Hayden Fry.

"I was interviewed by Iowa, but I was never offered the head coaching job," Stoops told me. "It's pretty simple. I was already offered the job at Oklahoma.

"In the end, when you're offered a job at a place and not the other place, you do what you feel is the right thing to do."

However, Stoops had no hard feelings about not receiving a coaching offer from Iowa.

"I have a great love for Iowa and the Iowa program," he said.

"It's very special to me. I'm always rooting for them. I think Kirk Ferentz is an excellent coach and is doing a great job.

"Believe me, I'm all for them and rooting for them hard."

From 0-8 to 8-0 in Big Ten

It took a while for Kirk Ferentz to get Iowa's football program rolling.

Ferentz had some people wondering if he was the right guy for the job when his first Hawkeye team in 1999 beat only Northern Illinois in an 11-game schedule and went 0-8 in the Big Ten.

COACH KIRK FERENTZ

Iowa showed some late-season improvement in 2000, winning in two overtimes at Penn State 26-23 and defeating Northwestern 27-17 the following week, but the overall record was only 3-9.

But better things came in 2001 when Iowa went 7-5 overall and 4-4 in the Big Ten and slipped past Texas Tech in the Alamo Bowl 19-16. Then came 2002 and the 11-2 season that saw Ferentz's team set a school record for victories and tie Ohio State for the Big Ten title with an 8-0 record.

Ferentz was named the Associated Press National Coach of the Year after being voted Big Ten Coach of the

Year and District Coach of the Year by the American Football Coaches Association before that.

"This has been an exciting year for all of us involved with the football program at the University of Iowa, and I am truly honored," Ferentz said after winning the AP award. "This is a reflection of all the hard work put forth by all of the members of our coaching staff and all of our players.

"I am pleased for everybody who has been a part of the team, that they may share in this recognition.

"For a team to go from 0-8 to 8-0 in the Big Ten is just a remarkable story. The entire process has been so enjoyable, and that is due to the people I work with every day. I've said before what a great situation I have here. I enjoying doing what I do, working with great people and being at the University of Iowa."

Said Iowa athletic director Bob Bowlsby: "I'm happy for Kirk, his staff and our football team. It has been a team effort on their part from the very start. Kirk and his staff represent the best in college athletics in the way they have built our program to earn the Big Ten Conference championship and Orange Bowl invitation. Kirk has been nothing short of exceptional in the job he has done representing the University of Iowa."

"Solid" is the Word for Ferentz

Solid.

That's how Iowa athletic director Bob Bowlsby describes Hawkeye football coach Kirk Ferentz.

"I feel very richly blessed to have Kirk as our coach," Bowlsby said. "Among the things that attracted me to him were his own demeanor and what people had to say about him in terms of what he stood for, how he handled things, and what was going to be important to him and what wasn't."

Ferentz's Hawkeyes were reeling off victory after victory, climbing steadily in the polls, when I talked with Bowlsby about his coach.

"What impressed you about him?" I asked.

"The same things that impress me about him now. He doesn't get very rattled, for the most part. He's very meticulous. He's probably a little more like Bill Snyder than Hayden Fry."

Snyder had been Iowa's offensive coordinator under Fry. He later became an outstanding head coach at Kansas State. Ferentz had been an Iowa offensive line coach.

One thing Bowlsby recalls was how Ferentz was criticized by fans shortly after he was hired.

"He got criticized because he appeared to go too slow in putting together his staff," Bowlsby explained. "He was very meticulous with who he looked at. He was very good at working with me on it, even though he was publicly criticized because he was supposed to have this instant staff and he didn't.

"That was indicative of how he looks at details. He wants to have the right chemistry. He made a very difficult decision on his strength and conditioning program, and he replaced a very popular guy. Now, four years later, he looks like a genius.

"Chris Doyle has established us as one of the most physical teams in the country. It was a tough decision for Kirk at the time, but he did it."

Ferentz "Pretty Green" as an Assistant

I asked Bump Elliott, who preceded Bob Bowlsby as Iowa's athletic director and was in the job from 1970-1991, if he could have predicted that Kirk Ferentz would, in 2002, coach the Hawkeyes to more victories in a season than anyone else in school history.

"I don't know if I did or didn't expect something like that," Elliott said. "When Kirk came in from Pittsburgh prior to the 1981 season to coach our offensive line, he was pretty green. I didn't know much about him.

"But the line played extremely well, and I would certainly give Kirk much of the credit for that. Also, Hayden Fry helped him a lot to be a good coach.

"At the time, we had assistant coaches such as Bill Snyder, Bill Brashier…quite a few good ones on the staff. To say that this one or that would be good head coaches, who knows?"

Ferentz remained at Iowa as the offensive line coach until taking the job as Maine's head coach prior to the 1990 season.

Ferentz Wouldn't Play "Blame Game"

Although Kirk Ferentz had trouble winning in his first two seasons as Iowa's football coach, he never played the "blame game."

So says Bob Brooks, the veteran broadcaster from Cedar Rapids, Iowa, who did play-by-play of Iowa's games for 55 years.

"In his first season, when he won only one game, I interviewed him after every loss and he stayed the course," Brooks said. "He never blamed Hayden Fry for anything, he never said, 'Hayden didn't leave me any players.'

"He never blamed the officials for bad calls. He never said he had bad luck. He never blamed the players. I told myself then, 'I'll bet he can do something.' And he's done it building block by building block.

"Now, after four seasons, he's had his best team. And that's kind of amazing because, when he opened his Big Ten season with a 49-3 loss at Michigan State in his first season in 1999, it looked like the Frank Lauterbur and Bob Commings eras. It was a mess. If you'd seen that game, you'd have asked, 'What are we getting into?'"

Brooks mentioned that "there had been a great hue and cry [by fans] to hire Bob Stoops as the coach." Ferentz obviously knew it.

"Kirk knew that Stoops was the golden boy, so to speak," Brooks said. "So what did Ferentz do? One of Stoops's children had a medical problem, and Bob had the work done at University Hospitals in Iowa City. While Stoops was in town, Ferentz had him go over and talk to his team."

"Go in There and Play Quarterback"

When Brad Banks was playing Little League football in Florida, his coach suddenly told him, "Go in there and play quarterback."

He did, and he's been doing it most of the time since.

And he's been doing it pretty well, too.

The way Banks looks at it, it was nice to be picked out to be a Little League quarterback, but that wasn't the important thing.

"I just wanted to play football," he explained. "I didn't care if I played offensive guard."

Well, OK, forget that offensive guard stuff now.

Banks, who was a 6'1", 200-pound senior from Belle Glade, Florida, was the starting quarterback when Iowa opened its season August 31, 2002 against Akron at Kinnick Stadium in Iowa City.

It was then that he stepped into the pressure cooker. Playing quarterback at Iowa and in most other major college programs brings with it a heavy amount of expectation from fans.

Banks saw it firsthand in the 2001 season. He was the backup to Kyle McCann, who then was the Hawkeyes' senior quarterback starter. Banks heard the outcry at Kinnick Stadium. He heard people who were dressed in Iowa black and gold booing.

Maybe they were booing McCann. Maybe they were booing Coach Kirk Ferentz for using McCann instead of Banks against Michigan. Maybe they were booing both McCann and Ferentz.

Whatever, it was an ugly situation on an afternoon when the Hawkeyes narrowly missed upsetting the Wolverines.

But Iowa got through it. McCann rose above the booing and helped Iowa to a 7-5 record that included a 19-16 victory over Texas Tech in the Alamo Bowl.

"It was kind of tough for Kyle to put up with stuff like that booing," Banks said. "We were all Hawkeyes."

Because of the fans' displeasure with McCann, Banks became a crowd favorite in 2001, and wound up his junior season with 41 pass completions in 68 attempts for 582 yards and four touchdowns. He ran 41 times for 151 yards and two touchdowns.

Brad Banks

Not Noticed—No Problem

Being the starter at quarterback on a major college football team in America is usually a high-profile situation.

Not so for Brad Banks of Iowa—at least early in his senior season.

Even though Banks became a clear-cut 2002 starter in spring practice, he was the first to admit he wasn't often recognized as Iowa's No. 1 quarterback while walking around the campus before the first game was played.

"But not being noticed doesn't bother me," he said.

He also said it didn't have any impact on him that he was Iowa's first black starting quarterback since Pete Gales, who lettered from 1978-1981.

Banks was surrounded by a horde of reporters as he patiently answered questions on Iowa's media day.

It was quite a difference from his days in junior college.

"On press day there, it was one guy, one camera, one microphone, five questions," he said with a smile.

Which situation did he like better?

"I kind of like this attention," he admitted.

Quarterback Turns Into Receiver

In August 2002, life changed in a big way for Clinton Solomon.

A year earlier, he was preparing to play for Eastern Hills High School in Fort Worth, Texas, which drew about 150 fans for its home games.

In late summer 2002, Solomon was preparing to be Iowa's second-team split end in the season opener against Akron. The game drew a crowd of 51,495 in 70,397-seat Kinnick Stadium.

Throughout most of his high school career, Solomon was a quarterback, and that's the position he was recruited for by Iowa's coaches. But in his first collegiate season, he was catching passes instead of throwing them.

Solomon indicated there should really be no mystery why he made the position switch.

"Yes, I was recruited as a quarterback, but as time went on I thought about it, and other guys thought playing receiver would be good for me," he explained. "I saw how many quarterbacks we have here, and I thought about the entire situation back home in Texas over the summer.

"So when I came here, I talked to Coach O'Keefe [Ken O'Keefe, Iowa's offensive coordinator and quarterbacks coach] and told him I preferred to be a receiver. I ran pass routes and worked on my speed during the summer, and didn't throw passes."

Solomon said such schools as Iowa State, Oklahoma and Oklahoma State were among others that showed interest in him.

In fact, he mistakenly said "Iowa State" when reviewing his recruiting trip to Iowa City that included watching a Big Ten basketball game.

When I asked him what game he saw, he began to say, "Iowa State against...."

Then he caught himself.

"I hate the Cyclones!" he said with a smile, perhaps thinking people expected him to say it. "The game I saw was Iowa against Penn State, and the crowd was unbelievable. I didn't make a visit to Iowa State, but they tried to recruit me as a secondary receiver.

"When it came down to choosing a college, I decided I wanted to leave Texas. I was impressed with the fan support, the coaching staff and education at Iowa."

593 Yards and Not One Punt

Not bad for openers.

Former coach Hayden Fry and ex-players Ed Podolak, Ray Jauch and Bernie Wyatt were among those who marveled at a 593-yard offensive barrage produced by Iowa in its August 31, 2002 season opener on Varsity Club Day.

The Hawkeyes made some mistakes, but still ran all over hopelessly outclassed Akron 57-21.

So overpowering was Iowa that it didn't have to punt all day.

"Oh, gosh, they were explosive!" said Jauch, a half-back on Hawkeye teams coached by Forest Evashevski in 1958, 1959 and 1960. "I think they have some great weapons on offense."

For those who don't consider it an official Iowa football season unless Fry—the Hawkeyes' coach from 1979-1998—is in the stadium, they got what they wanted. Fry, too, was impressed with the job done by a team coached by Kirk Ferentz, one of his former assistants.

Asked his thoughts of the Hawkeyes, Podolak—the standout Iowa back from 1966-1968 and now a veteran radio commentator on games involving his alma mater—said all someone had to do was look back two seasons.

"In 2000, we lost to Western Michigan—a Mid-American Conference team—by a 27-21 score," he explained. "Now, here we are, ready to be accused of running up the score against Akron.

"The improvement is outstanding in Iowa's offensive line, which is the key. Most of them have played together for three or four years. They're like a well-oiled machine."

Wyatt, who lettered as a halfback from 1959-1961, watched the game from the Iowa sideline. The former Iowa and Wisconsin assistant coach was the Hawkeyes' honorary captain for the Akron game.

He liked what he saw.

"Ever since Kirk Ferentz got here, the thing that has always impressed me is that his teams play real hard and they're tough kids," Wyatt said. "Now it's just a matter of getting a few more athletes, and that will happen.

"The more you win, the better the recruiting goes for you. They do a great job here, they work hard and they're tough."

Iowa State Rivalry Tough for Greving

"It's been hard. Really hard."

So said Aaron Greving.

Iowa was fresh from a 29-24 victory over Miami of Ohio, but several days remained before Greving and the

Hawkeyes would play in-state rival Iowa State at Kinnick Stadium in 2002.

Greving, who had begun the season as Iowa's No. 1 running back but was hampered by an ankle injury, was standing in the afternoon sunshine outside the Hayden Fry Football Complex in Iowa City—talking about Iowa's recent frustration against Iowa State.

The thing that made it even more difficult for Greving to accept than perhaps some of the other Hawkeyes was that he was from Ames, where Iowa State is located.

"I never thought I'd be around to see Iowa State beat Iowa—and now it's happened four times in a row," Greving said. "One of my goals when I came here was to beat Iowa State every time, but it hasn't happened.

"But I still have two games left, and I'll see what I can do to turn that around."

Greving said he "considered going to Iowa State when I was a high school freshman, but I began talking with Iowa's coaches after my sophomore year. I committed to Iowa in my senior year.

"The Iowa State coaches were kind of angry that I didn't go there. I don't blame anyone for not liking me for not going there, but that's a decision I made. Iowa City has been the best place for me, and it's been a great experience.

Unfortunately, the Greving story did not have a happy ending.

The 207-pound junior who began the season as Iowa's No. 1 running back, left the team as it was in the week of preparation for the game at Michigan.

"Aaron's battled significant injury problems since the spring, and at this time feels he needs a break from football," Coach Kirk Ferentz said.

In-State Emotions Run High

Everyone knew where Iowa middle linebacker Fred Barr stood on the Hawkeyes' rivalry with Iowa State.

"I hate them," Barr said as the game approached.

Frustrated after four consecutive losses Iowa had suffered in the series, Barr said, "I'm expecting to win. We've been the underdogs my whole time here going into this [2002] game. But we're a good team. So we should be favored."

Indeed, the Hawkeyes were favored—by four points.

It also pained Iowa strong safety Bob Sanders that Iowa State had been dominating the rivalry.

"It hurt real bad to see the seniors leave last year without winning in the series," the junior said.

"A lot of guys were down after we lost at Ames in November [2001].

"It was a horrible feeling, and it's not something I want to go through again. I feel it's time for us to win."

Sanders said he hoped the Hawkeyes in the 2002 game would be stronger than they were in the 17-14 loss at Ames on November 24, 2001. The game was delayed because of the September 11 terrorist attacks.

Fifth Straight Loss to Iowa State

Despite Barr's "I hate them" words and the "horrible" feeling Sanders had, Iowa State kept its streak going against Iowa in 2002.

The Cyclones made it five straight in the series with a 36-31 victory before a capacity crowd of 70,397 at Kinnick Stadium on September 14.

No one savored the Cyclones' victory more than Zach Butler, the 292-pound senior center from Iowa City.

"Unbelievable!" Butler said after Iowa State stormed back from a 24-7 halftime deficit to win. "I'm the happiest guy you'll ever meet. Five in a row over Iowa...and I couldn't be more proud to be associated with the Iowa State Cyclones and Coach Dan McCarney for giving me the opportunity to play here.

"It was probably the biggest victory I've ever had as a Cyclone. Iowa came out fired up and ready to go. They had something to prove because they hadn't won against us for four years.

"I love playing against Iowa and I love the competition. There was no greater feeling walking out as a captain in my hometown. I don't hate Iowa. I respect them very much. They have a great ball club.

"Coach Kirk Ferentz has done a great job. I'll tell you what, they're going to be battling for the Big Ten title, and we all know that."

Little did anyone know then how prophetic Butler would turn out to be. Iowa didn't lose a Big Ten game and shared the championship with Ohio State.

No Censorship

Coach Kirk Ferentz said he didn't run "a pure dictatorship" at Iowa.

He made that comment after being asked about some of the things his players had been saying in 2002—specifically the—"I hate them" statement Fred Barr made about Iowa State several days before the game was played.

Fearing such comments would provide the next opponent—especially in an emotional rivalry like Iowa-Iowa State—with bulletin-board material, some coaches would fly into a rage.

However, Ferentz indicated he didn't want to control everything his athletes did or said.

If one of his Hawkeyes said he didn't particularly care for the opposing team, Ferentz said he wouldn't throw a fit.

"I'm not going to censor our players," he said. "That's part of growing up. I give advice to players and they take it where they want.

"If you say you don't like the opposition…why would you [like the opposition]? That's stating the obvious."

What It's Like to Coach a Son

After Aaron Greving quit the team and Fred Russell was injured, Iowa coach Kirk Ferentz was trying to figure out who would start at running back against Wisconsin late in the 2002 season.

Suddenly, a reporter asked about Brian Ferentz, the coach's son and a reserve center who had injured a knee at midseason.

"We were not going to use Brian at running back anyway," Kirk Ferentz said. "He's like his old man—his speed is not too good. So there's a little bit of a problem."

Ferentz is the first Iowa coach to have his son on the team since Bobby Commings lettered as an Iowa quarterback in 1977 and 1978 while playing for his father, Bob Sr.

Bobby made his dad proud by having a sizeable role in Iowa's 12-10 victory over Iowa State in 1977—the first time the teams played after a 43-year lapse in the series.

I asked Kirk Ferentz what it's like to coach his son, and he said it's generally been positive.

"It started with the recruitment process," the coach said. "He had a decision to make, as did we. We made ours; then I think his was more important. His was probably more important to him because he has his peer groups to deal with. The big thing is there's enough insulation between us where I'm not day-to-day or hour-to-hour with him. I'm not making a lot of critiques of what he's doing.

"In coaching, you miss so much of your kids, so selfishly it's fun to walk onto the field—not that I'm watching all the time—and see him. It's kind of neat to walk through the [football] building and see him every now and then. He'll sneak into my office occasionally and we'll have a quick conversation."

During the season, Kirk said, his son comes by the family home on most Sundays.

"That's one time when the whole family sits down and visits," he said. "But I'm also sure he goes home when I don't know about it."

Hinkel Said "No" to Penn State Scholarship

I can tell you for a fact that legendary Penn State coach Joe Paterno does *not* get every football player he wants.

I know because Ed Hinkel told me so.

When Hinkel was a student at Cathedral Prep High School in Erie, Pennsylvania—three hours from the Penn State campus—Paterno said he had a scholarship for him.

Hinkel had a surprise for him.

He didn't accept it.

He enrolled at Iowa instead.

"It was a hard decision to make," Hinkel said. "Basically, it came down to me deciding that Iowa was the best fit for me."

In the recruiting process, Hinkel said, "Penn State kind of jumped in late on me. Coach Ferentz and his staff were actually the first to offer me a scholarship. They were there the whole way with me, so that's one of the reasons I'm a Hawkeye."

Hinkel, a 6'1", 170-pound wide receiver, said he finally made his decision to choose Iowa over Penn State a week before the signing date. Before playing in the Hawkeyes' game at Penn State as a redshirt freshman in 2002, Hinkel said he had been in 107,282-seat Beaver Stadium for only one other game.

"I went there as a Penn State recruit, but I actually talked to Coach Ferentz on the sidelines there," he explained.

"I was kind of cheering for Iowa, but I had no clue then where I was going to school. It was a great experience, being a Pennsylvania guy and seeing that Iowa could go into Penn State and win a football game."

The November 4, 2000 game was perhaps the most exciting in the 17-game series. Iowa won 26-23 in two overtimes.

Asked if that was something that helped convince him to accept Iowa's scholarship offer, Hinkel said, "Yes, a little bit. I never heard of Iowa until they started recruiting me. I did dream of playing at Penn State [at one time], but things just didn't work out. Now I'm playing here."

Asked if his decision to leave Pennsylvania and head west to Iowa was popular with his family and friends, Hinkel said, "Everybody supported me. Wherever I chose to go, people were wishing me the best of luck."

Hinkel said he twice visited with Paterno during the recruiting process.

"It was tough to tell Penn State that I wasn't going there," he said. "I didn't actually tell Coach Paterno. I told assistant coach Tom Bradley. I knew they were pretty upset that I decided to come to Iowa."

"My Mom Will Be a Nervous Wreck"

As the Iowa-Penn State game approached in 2002, Hawkeye wide receiver Ed Hinkel was asked how his parents—Peggy and Mike Hinkel of Erie, Pennsylvania—would react while watching the game.

"My mom probably will be going nuts," Hinkel said. "She'll be a nervous wreck. I mean, she really isn't one to be able to handle a lot of pressure. She says she doesn't know how she's going to make it through four years of me standing back there catching punts.

"My dad is a pretty calm guy, so he'll probably be fine with it."

In the game, Hinkel caught two passes for 28 yards—one a 22-yarder for a touchdown in the second quarter. He also returned a punt for 54 yards.

"Pain in the Butt"

The game against Iowa State, of course, was big for the players from Iowa on the Hawkeyes' roster.

But Coach Kirk Ferentz, who attended high school in Pittsburgh, said he got no particular thrill out of competing against Penn State.

"Not at all," Ferentz said. "It's kind of a pain in the butt. When it's your state, you get more ticket requests. And I hate the ticket business. I'm not into the ticket business. I let others handle that. That part of it is a little bit of a nuisance. But, again, I don't let it be a nuisance in my life.

"If I were playing, [the Iowa-Penn State] game might be a factor. Fortunately for us, I'm not playing."

Fasten Your Seat Belts

More proof that fans had to fasten their seat belts while watching Iowa in 2002 came in its Big Ten opener at Penn State.

The Hawkeyes somehow let a 22-point lead vanish in the last eight minutes before snapping back to win 42-35 in overtime at State College, Pennsylvania.

"Just thinking about the game gives me goosebumps," said Iowa defensive back Derek Pagel.

Iowa owned a 35-13 lead heading into the fourth quarter, but was outscored 22-0 in the final 15 minutes of regulation time.

The victory over a Penn State team then ranked 12th nationally was the Hawkeyes' first on the road over a ranked foe since 1996—and that foe was Penn State, which then was ranked eighth.

Brad Banks, who wound up throwing four touchdown passes, hit C. J. Jones on a six-yarder for the decisive play in overtime.

Coach Kirk Ferentz said he had wanted to use the play earlier in the game, "but I chickened out. That's why I'm not the offensive coordinator."

Another Honor for Gilliam

Frank Gilliam, who had been a standout end at Iowa in the 1950s and was later named to the university's All-Century team, came back to be an honorary captain in 2002.

He spoke to the team the day before the Hawkeyes' game against Michigan State on October 12, went to the center of the field with Iowa's captains for the pregame coin flip, and watched the game from the press box.

Iowa made it a very pleasant experience for him by cruising past the Spartans, 44-16.

"I was honored to spend the weekend here," Gilliam said. "I talked to the Iowa players Friday night. I told them of my feelings about the University of Iowa, I told them what I thought of the program here and how well they were playing.

"I told them I had confidence in them and I wished them luck."

Gilliam was serving as a senior consultant for player personnel for the Minnesota Vikings after a longtime administrative career with that team. Before going to the NFL job, Gilliam had been an assistant coach on Ray Nagel's staff at Iowa from 1966-1970.

Did I Put a Hex on the Hawkeyes?

I've got to admit it.

For a long time on the day Iowa played Purdue in 2002, I was afraid Mike Reilly and I had put a hex on the Hawkeyes.

I was standing on the radio and TV level in the press box at Kinnick Stadium, waiting to join the broadcast team of play-by-play radio announcer Gary Dolphin and commentator Ed Podolak for a few minutes of first-half air time.

Dolphin had invited me to talk about this book—which I then was in the process of writing—over the vast Iowa network.

Before donning the headset and microphone, I talked briefly with Reilly, a guard who was Iowa's most valuable player in 1963. He played for Jerry Burns's teams in 1961, 1962 and 1963.

Reilly, always a witty guy, said, "Hey, Ron, do you think those four Big Ten referees who were fired this week have been assigned to this game?"

I thought it was a funny line because it appeared the refs had taken over the Iowa-Purdue game. They threw more yellow flags and walked off more penalties early in the game than I had seen in any stadium all season.

Three days earlier, the Big Ten had disciplined four officials for what commissioner Jim Delany called work "that did not meet Big Ten standards. Therefore, they will forfeit future officiating assignments."

The zebras who were disciplined had worked the Wake Forest-Purdue game two weeks before the Iowa-Purdue game.

So, as I was wrapping up my appearance on the air with Dolphin and Podolak, I said something like, "Hey, our old buddy, Mike Reilly, just guaranteed himself a spot in the book. He said he wondered if the four referees who were disciplined by the Big Ten were assigned to this game."

Afterward, I began to wonder if the comment about the lousy officiating in the Iowa-Purdue game—and what Reilly and I said about it—was going to cast a dark cloud over Iowa's homecoming game, which was being played in bright sunshine.

Did the officials somehow hear what Reilly said about them and what I repeated on the radio network?

No, I finally told myself. I was just being paranoid.

But for what seemed an eternity, the officiating got no better and neither did the Hawkeyes' performance.

They fell behind 14-3 in the second quarter, and they were penalized a whopping nine times for 80 yards in the first half. Purdue, meanwhile, was penalized three times for 28 yards in the opening 30 minutes.

Interestingly, Iowa (which moved its records to 5-1 overall and 2-0 in the Big Ten against Purdue) wasn't called for one penalty in the last half and stormed back to win 31-28 on Brad Banks's seven-yard touchdown pass with 1:09 remaining.

All Those Close Finishes

Despite being outgained in total yardage, 507-384, and outplayed much of the game by Purdue, Iowa dodged a huge bullet.

By that time, the Hawkeyes had so many close finishes in the 2002 season that running back Fred Russell was asked if there was any reason that fans needed to show up before the fourth quarter.

"We make it tight," said Russell, who led all rushers with 121 yards in 22 carries against the Boilermakers. "When we had a 10-point lead, I tried to remind everybody that we still had one quarter to play.

"We had already seen one game slip away [a 36-31 loss to Iowa State] and almost another [a 42-35 victory in overtime at Penn State]."

After arriving in the interview room, Iowa athletic director Bob Bowlsby said, "I need a physical."

So did a lot of other people.

It was that kind of day.

Iowa's Fan Support

Bobby Williams, who was in his final season as Michigan State's coach in 2002, said Iowa's fans "do a tremendous job of getting behind their team. The atmosphere there is just outstanding. The crowd noise makes it hard for opposing teams.

"A lot of stadiums are like that, but this one [at Iowa] stands out. Regardless of the situation they're in, they get tremendous support from the fans."

A 21-16 decision over Michigan State in 2000 gave Ferentz his first Big Ten victory.

Temporary Parking?

You know how it sometimes goes in college football.

When your team is winning—but isn't ranked—the coach, players and fans call it a lack of respect.

When your team is winning and the team starts rising in the rankings and in the eyes of the nation, the players and fans love it and the coach says, "Not so fast!"

Well, Iowa's Kirk Ferentz was looking at it this way after his team had a 5-1 record overall and was 2-0 in the Big Ten in 2002: He's calling it "temporary parking right now."

Asked if he realistically felt his team would be ranked in the top 20 in the relatively short amount of time he'd been the coach, Ferentz said, "It's premature to get too excited about anything that's going on with the conference race or the national race.

"We still have six games remaining in the conference. That's really where our thoughts are at this point."

Ferentz said he had "no preconceived notions about anything" as talk of Iowa being a Rose Bowl contender mounted.

"I try to keep it that way," Ferentz said. "Our philosophy is to put an honest day's work into it. I knew I was coming into a great situation at Iowa. Being here [as an assistant] for nine years under Coach Hayden Fry, I knew what a great place this was and how great the people are.

"I was very confident and I remain confident that we're going to have our share of success if we do things right."

Quarter in the Meter

Ferentz's comment about Iowa being in "temporary parking" atop the Big Ten standings came up again a couple of weeks later after its records in 2002 soared to 4-0 in the Big Ten and 7-1 overall.

Asked what kind of parking pass those achievements gave the Hawkeyes, Ferentz said, "We might have a quarter in the meter instead of a nickel or a dime."

Naturally, the conservative Ferentz wasn't ready to start making up a room list for his players in Pasadena.

Not with Iowa's game at Michigan (6-1 and 3-0) just around the corner.

"Look around," he said. "Things change so much in college football. It's the nature of conference play. There's still a lot of football to be played. We still have a lot of football left after this one is over."

No Band-Aid Approach

In his first coaching term at Iowa, as an assistant under Hayden Fry from 1981-1989, Kirk Ferentz was in charge of the offensive line.

After he'd been Iowa's head coach for more than three years, Ferentz was asked if he took a "trenches-first" approach to his recruiting when he got to Iowa City as Fry's successor.

"I'm assuming you're talking about our line," Ferentz answered. "I don't believe you can win consistently at any level—high school, college or the NFL—without top line play on both sides of the football.

"We were a little deficient in that area when I got here, and we had some guys who had gotten career-ending injuries and some guys who had transferred out. For whatever reason, we weren't experienced or strong up front on both sides of the ball.

"It's been a focus. Anybody going into a new situation tries to improve weaknesses and tries to play to the strengths. The biggest thing was we didn't look for a Band-Aid approach, and hopefully that will pay off for us down the road."

How Do You Measure Toughness?

After Iowa began reeling off victory after victory in 2002, someone mentioned to Coach Kirk Ferentz that the team's "toughness" was showing as it approached its game against Michigan.

Michigan State coach Bobby Williams, whose team lost to Iowa 44-16, said the Hawkeyes' offensive linemen were "by far the most physical we've faced. They have some guys with tremendous height, size and upper-body strength."

As for Ferentz?

"How do you measure toughness?" he asked. "I don't know how you measure toughness. It's like, how do you motivate players? The best answer I've heard is that you surround yourself with motivated players when you recruit them. If you're in the NFL, you try to draft them.

"I'll never forget when I came to Iowa in 1981. People said Iowa didn't have the greatest teams in the

1960s and 1970s, but those who had been around then said Iowa had a tradition of working hard and playing tough.

"That's been a tradition at our place. As long as we wear equipment in football, those are going to be real important things—work ethic and toughness. If you can get better through hard work, you have a chance to have a decent team."

Then the subject of talent came up. Ferentz was asked if Iowa's talent measured up to the level of Michigan's.

"Oh, I don't know about that," he responded. "You watch recruiting stuff year in and year out. Typically, Michigan gets the best recruiting class year in and year out in the Big Ten. We're playing a very talented football team, a very gifted team.

"I don't know if we have enough talent to measure up."

Similarities Between 2002 and the 1980s

Michigan coach Lloyd Carr saw a similarity between Hayden Fry's strong teams in the 1980s and Iowa under Kirk Ferentz in 2002.

"Kirk was the offensive line coach for Hayden in the 1980s, and those Iowa teams then had big, strong, dominating offensive lines and defensive fronts that were very physical," Carr said. "Those teams took great pride in the kicking game and being physically tough."

Carr also took note of Brad Banks, the Iowa quarterback who became one of the Big Ten's best as a senior in 2002.

"Banks has a great arm," Carr said. "He has hit seven or eight passes of 50 yards or more. He has the ability off play action to make deep throws. The big-play capability he presents is the reason they're second in the nation in scoring at 40 points a game."

Russell's Emergence

Fred Russell's bust-out as one of the nation's best collegiate running backs was even more evident as Iowa swung into its stretch run in the 2002 Big Ten race.

"I'm not familiar with the other guys around the country," Coach Kirk Ferentz said, "but Fred's emergence has been great for us. And we're not totally surprised. If you'd asked me last January, I'd have told you he was one of our most improved football players over the last 15 months—if not the most improved.

"He hasn't done anything since then to regress. He's learned to be a complete player, not just a runner. His performance is a reflection of his work ethic and his attention to detail, and he's a guy who really loves the game."

It turned out that Ferentz knew nothing about Russell when he visited Milford Academy in Connecticut on a recruiting trip.

"It's kind of funny," Ferentz said. "All the time you spend, all the money you spend and the thinking that goes into recruiting. I actually was going in to visit with a young man who's now playing for Purdue.

"He had already committed to Purdue, but his coach said, 'Hey, we have a young man here who you might want to talk to.' It just happened to be Fred Russell.

"That's how the ball got rolling. The next thing you know, he was on our campus and liked what he saw."

Russell is listed as a 5'8", 185-pound junior from Inkster, Michigan.

That 5'8" might be stretching it.

No problem with the height, Ferentz indicated.

"We're Iowa," he explained. "It's not like we're in an amusement park, where you have those bars and you have to be so tall to ride a ride.

"We don't have that here. We're just looking for good players, and Fred is a good player. Bob Sanders isn't bad, either."

Sanders is listed as a 5'8", 200-pound defensive back. Again, the 5'8" might be stretching it.

"As long as we don't have to play basketball against whoever we're going to play, I think we're OK," Ferentz said.

Don't Mention Michigan

Shhh.

Don't mention Michigan.

When Iowa had a 6-1 record in 2002, heading into a game at Indiana, Coach Kirk Ferentz warned his players.

He told them if he heard any of them mentioning the Michigan game, which was held the following week, they wouldn't be on the traveling squad to Indiana.

"If anybody is even thinking about that, they're just flat-out dumb—too dumb to play for us," Ferentz said.

The warning must have paid off. The Hawkeyes, who got three pass interceptions from linebacker Grant Steen, rolled past Indiana 24-8 to set up a showdown at Michigan the following week.

Taking the Quiz

Multiple-choice question:

Q. What's the best way an Iowa football fan can spend a Saturday afternoon?

(a) Attending a game at Michigan Stadium on October 26, 2002

(b) Watching Michigan's fans start filing out of the place in the third quarter

(c) Being able to hold up a "Rose Bowl" sign and not be accused of spiking your Pepsi with something stronger

(d) Watching the Hawkeye quarterback take a knee in the fourth quarter

(e) All of the above

The correct answer is "e."

Brad Banks threw three touchdown passes as Iowa ended a string of seven consecutive losses to Michigan with a 34-9 victory before 111,496 fans—the largest crowd ever to see a Hawkeye team play. It was Michigan's worst home loss since 1967.

However, it turned out the Rose Bowl sign meant nothing. Iowa wound up going to the Orange Bowl and not the Rose Bowl after the regular season ended.

"Distraction Week"

Although Coach Kirk Ferentz was pleased with the maturity his players were showing after they improved their 2002 records to 8-1 overall and 5-0 in the Big Ten by thrashing Michigan, he was concerned with the distractions that might influence them.

As a game against Wisconsin approached, Ferentz said, "I'm not as worried about 'letdown week' as I am 'distraction week.' They probably coincide a little. This will be another big test. The Wisconsin game will be every bit as tough as the Michigan game.

"It's good for fans to be caught up in [the late-season excitement], but our players can't be fans. They need to be football players."

Asked what he meant by distractions, Ferentz said, "Right now, what's everybody writing about? I assume bowl games...that kind of stuff. It's like preseason stuff. And preseason stuff doesn't mean anything, either. There's so much football yet to be played, so many variables."

Still on the subject of distractions, Ferentz talked about a situation he witnessed firsthand when he was on the Cleveland Browns' coaching staff in 1995.

"Going into that season, we were picked to be Super Bowl representatives from the AFC side by *Sports Illustrated*," he said. "We were 12-6 the year before. Then, after eight to 10 weeks, it was announced the franchise would be moving [to Baltimore].

"The team flat-out quit performing. Quit playing. It was one of the most disastrous, distasteful things I've ever been through as a coach.

"You go from, hey, we're going to the Super Bowl to that. So what people say in August doesn't mean anything. And what is being written about our team now [in the final week of October 2002] has no bearing on this Iowa team."

Just Two Stoplights

Bruce Nelson was talking about stoplights.

"We have two of them in my whole county," the Iowa center said. "Steiny probably has stoplights at each end of his block."

"Steiny" was Eric Steinbach, the left guard who played alongside Nelson in the Hawkeyes' standout offensive line in 2002.

The 6'7", 284-pound Steinbach was from New Lenox, Illinois, and was having another outstanding season after being named a first-team all-Big Ten player by coaches in 2001.

The 6'4", 290-pound Nelson was from Emmetsburg, Iowa, and had become a starter after arriving at Iowa as a non-scholarship player.

The stoplights Nelson was talking about—both of them in Palo Alto County—were in Emmetsburg.

Busy streets or not, Nelson was proud to be from Emmetsburg.

"There isn't a better place to grow up in," he said. "There's a great high school football tradition there. It's a fabulous program. Kids dream about playing for the Hawkeyes there.

"I weighed my options when I was thinking about college. I received phone calls and letters from the Hawkeyes and other Division I schools, but when it came to signing day, I wasn't able to get a scholarship. Lots of players from Emmetsburg have gone to places like South Dakota and South Dakota State, and I thought about that, too.

"But I wanted to see if I could play for the Hawkeyes. I figured that if it didn't work out, I could transfer to a smaller school. I grew up wearing Hawkeye black and gold and didn't want to change when I went to college."

Another small-town Iowan in the Hawkeyes' offensive line was 6'7", 300-pound tackle Robert Gallery of Masonville.

"We catch a lot of grief from the Chicago guys by being from small-town Iowa," Nelson said. "But we certainly can play with them, so we throw that back in their faces. Eric Steinbach loves to brag about Chicago and how they have the best football, but I think he understands that football is football.

"We have a good time with it. That's what makes it so much fun to know each other. We've jelled being from different places."

As you would expect, there were a number of different personalities among the offensive linemen.

Tough Weekend for Announcers

The last weekend of October 2002 was a tough one for two former longtime play-by-play announcers of University of Iowa sports events.

Gene Claussen, 81, died October 26 in Iowa City of complications of a stroke. Claussen earned a degree from Iowa and had been a broadcaster for 40 years. He had owned station KXIC in Iowa City.

Jim Zabel, 81, was hospitalized in Des Moines the day after Claussen's death after being involved in a head-on collision. Zabel was a longtime play-by-play announcer for Iowa football and basketball games on station WHO in Des Moines.

How Nice Would It Be?

For a number of years, Kirk Ferentz, Dan McCarney, Barry Alvarez and Bill Snyder had a common goal.

That goal was to help coach Iowa to football victories over other teams. All had been assistants on Hayden Fry's Hawkeye staff before heading in different directions.

Ferentz eventually came back to be Iowa's head coach in 1999, where he had problems beating McCarney (who was Iowa State's head coach), Alvarez (who was Wisconsin's head coach) and Snyder (who was Kansas State's head coach).

Before the Iowa-Wisconsin game in 2002, Ferentz was asked how nice it would be to beat one of coaches with whom he was on the Iowa staff with in the 1980s.

"That's a nice way of saying I'm 0 for all three of them," Ferentz responded. "That's very tactful. I appreciate that."

At the time, Ferentz was 0 for eight against McCarney, Alvarez and Snyder. McCarney had beaten him four times, Alvarez three times and Snyder once.

But the Iowa coach ended his losing streak by beating Alvarez's Wisconsin team 20-3 on November 2, 2002.

Dallas Clark: A Huge Success Story

Dallas Clark was a classic "Small-Town-Player-Makes-Good-At-The-Big-University" story.

Clark was a 6'4", 244-pounder from tiny Livermore, Iowa, who came to Iowa without a football scholarship.

Originally, he hoped to be a big-time linebacker, but Coach Kirk Ferentz talked him into being a tight end—and in 2002 I felt there wasn't a better one in the Big Ten Conference.

"Livermore is 30 miles north of Fort Dodge and has a population of a little more than 400," Clark told me after catching five passes in Iowa's 20-3 victory over Wisconsin on November 2, 2002. "It takes about seven towns to make up my high school."

The high school Clark attended was Twin River Valley of Bode, which is five miles from Livermore.

Clark earned four letters in football, basketball and track and five in baseball at Twin River Valley.

"I played quarterback and linebacker there," he said. "I ran the high and low hurdles in track, but we didn't actually have a track at the school. We practiced on the football field, and all of our meets were away from home.

"On rainy days when I'd practice the hurdles on the football field, it was kind of scary. I didn't want to kill myself."

Clark said he came to Iowa without a scholarship because "I always wanted to play Division I and Iowa was the only Division I school interested in me. It sounded like they'd give me an honest chance."

He said he had "big dreams" and "a lot of goals to make big plays" as an Iowa linebacker.

"But Coach Ferentz came to me and asked if I wanted to play tight end," he said. "I've been timed electronically in the 40 at 4.66 seconds, and—after a year—I said I'd switch positions."

Clark Would Give Heisman to Banks

Although Iowa quarterback Brad Banks was regarded as an also-ran in the Heisman Trophy derby late in the 2002 season, Hawkeye tight end Dallas Clark said, "I'd vote for him. He's our guy.

"Why wouldn't you have 100 percent confidence in him? Right now he's performing better than anyone, and I'm glad he's on our team."

So was Coach Kirk Ferentz.

Ferentz had been reluctant to say much about Banks deserving national honors, but after Banks had another strong game against Wisconsin, Ferentz said, "I know this—he's All-Iowa. We're definitely not trading Brad Banks for anybody.

DALLAS CLARK

"I know he's done a great job of leading our team. He personifies our whole team. If we do a good job, if he plays well, he'll probably get the honors he deserves."

Banks said he wasn't thinking about the Heisman Trophy, adding that any such talk by others wasn't a distraction to him.

"I don't let it go to my head," he said.

Another thing Iowa's players weren't letting get to their heads were the roses that some people were carrying inside and outside Kinnick Stadium the day they beat Wisconsin 20-3.

That's r-o-s-e-s, as in Rose Bowl.

"It's good to see the fans excited," Clark said. "We had a great atmosphere for the game. There were tons of people, and they saw a good game."

But Clark was quick to add that there were no roses in the Hawkeyes' locker room.

"You guys have interviewed how many people?" he asked. "Do you think Coach Ferentz is going to let anything like that in our locker room? No. Never. We've got Northwestern to get ready for now."

Pressure on Every Kick

"I'm the type of player who puts a lot of pride into, and pressure on, every kick," said Iowa placekicker Nate Kaeding.

Kaeding's streak of consecutive field goal successes ended at 22 when he missed a 27-yarder in the third quarter against Wisconsin in 2002.

"I hit it pretty well, but left it too far to the right," said Kaeding, who connected on field goals of 32 and 30 yards before missing the 27-yarder.

Kaeding said he regards the pressure to succeed as being equal on every attempt—"whether it's a 27-yarder when we're up by 14 points or a 48-yarder with 40 seconds left to win a bowl game."

Kaeding said it's sometimes difficult to imagine how things have changed in the Iowa football picture in recent seasons.

"I'd be sitting here when I was a freshman two years ago [when Iowa's record was 3-9] and to be thinking we'd be playing for the Rose Bowl and to be undefeated in the Big Ten...well, I'd have never had that thought," he said.

"Something Historical"

Maurice "Mo" Brown caught six passes for 107 yards to lead Iowa's receivers against Wisconsin.

It marked the fourth time in the 2002 season that Brown had eclipsed 100 yards in a game.

Said Brown when asked how he felt about the possibility of being on a team that could win more games than any previous one at Iowa: "That's beautiful. It's a great feeling that I'm part of a team that can do something historical."

Bill Snyder Lauds Ferentz

Bill Snyder went on to a wonderful career as Kansas State's head coach after doing a fine job as Hayden Fry's offensive coordinator at Iowa from 1979-1988.

Long after Snyder moved from Iowa City to Manhattan, Kansas, he recalled the young offensive line coach—Kirk Ferentz—who joined Fry's staff in 1981.

"I know all of us have a great appreciation for our opportunities to be with Hayden and each other," Snyder said in recalling his years with Fry. "I'm excited about how well each of them are doing. I'm excited about Kirk Ferentz at the University of Iowa.

"You know, there was some criticism over that hire…But Kirk has an unbelievably talented approach to the game of football, how he coaches people and how he teaches the game."

The "criticism" Snyder was referring to centered around the wishes of the sizeable number of Iowa fans that the successor to Fry should have been Bob Stoops, the former Iowa player who went on to do a sensational job as Oklahoma's head coach.

But…

Snyder said Ferentz is "one of those guys that you know is always going to be successful. I go back to when we first had the opportunity to hire Kirk [at Iowa]. I think he was a volunteer or part-time coach [at Pittsburgh]. It seemed like a little bit of a risk, but in his first year there we went to the Rose Bowl and won the Big Ten title.

"He was as instrumental in the success as anyone.

"Barry Alvarez [another former Fry staff member], of course, is doing well as Wisconsin's head coach. We always talk about the fact that maybe the best of all was Bill Brashier, who stayed on as defensive coordinator and retired at the University of Iowa.

"Unfortunately, he was never given the opportunity to do some of the things we do. He was probably the most talented of all."

"Why Would I Want to Leave?"

With Iowa continuing to win late in the 2002 season, it was natural for fans and reporters to start wondering if the name of Kirk Ferentz might start sounding attractive to those seeking to hire coaches for collegiate or National Football League jobs.

"Why would I want to leave?" Ferentz asked "That's my approach. I've got a great job. I've got a great situation."

The summer before the 2002 season began, Ferentz's contract was extended and his salary was guaranteed at $910,000 a year. He also was due to receive incentive bonuses.

Ferentz said his name being linked to other jobs wasn't "something I spend a lot of time thinking about. I know it's going to be out there. And I know we're going to have to diffuse some situations."

Indeed, Ferentz was interviewed after the season for the Jacksonville Jaguars' job in the NFL. Although he wasn't offered the Jacksonville job, Ferentz got another pay raise from Iowa and remained the Hawkeyes' coach.

"I'm an Emotional Person"

On the sideline during Iowa's wonderful 2002 season, Coach Kirk Ferentz seemed rock-solid.

Very little outward emotion. Very little change of expression.

But sometimes looks are deceiving.

After the Hawkeyes' 62-10 victory over Northwestern in their final home game, Ferentz showed his emotional side.

It had been Senior Day at Kinnick Stadium, and a crowd of 68,738 showed its appreciation.

So did Ferentz.

"Believe it or not, I'm an emotional person," he said. "Senior Day is always tough on me. It always has been."

Most of these seniors were guys who struggled with the 1-10 season in 1999 and the 3-9 season in 2000—Ferentz's first two years as Hayden Fry's successor.

Crushing Northwestern enabled the seniors and the others on Ferentz's fourth Hawkeye team to push their overall record to 10-1 and their Big Ten record to 7-0 heading into the regular-season finale at Minnesota.

Ferentz had five senior offensive linemen make a curtain call in the last half. The players held hands as they left the home field for the last time.

The players were emotionally moved. Obviously, so was their coach.

There Was No Quit in Big Ben

One of the Iowa seniors who ran off the Kinnick Stadium field for the last time in the 2002 home finale was Ben Sobieski.

Big Ben was quite a story.

"I've definitely come full-circle, and it's really been a long haul," the 6'5", 305-pounder said after the Hawkeyes clobbered Northwestern 62-10.

Sobieski had been around the Iowa football program for so long that it's a wonder people weren't asking him what it was like to block for the legendary Nile Kinnick in 1939.

It wouldn't have surprised me if other guys in some of his classes were asking him how it felt to play for Coach Forest Evashevski's Big Ten championship team at Iowa.

In 2002, Sobieski was a sixth-year player after being one of four true freshmen to start for Hayden Fry's 1997 team.

The one-time Parade and SuperPrep All-American battled injury after injury and admitted he was "on the edge of quitting quite a few times" because of the frustration.

But there was no quit in Big Ben.

"Even though I had some very difficult times, when it came down to it I've always had people supporting me," Sobieski said. "I always knew my best option—pretty much my only good option—was to stay here and give it my best. It's definitely been worth it.

"The offensive line is definitely a close group, and they've supported me a lot. When I wasn't playing, they were behind me. When I started to come back, they were behind me.

"I've had so many more downs than ups the last few years. But this year has definitely been worth it. It's the most fun I've ever had."

Sobieski, who was on the second team, knew he'd have plenty of family members and friends attending his regular-season finale the following Saturday at Minnesota, and he said it was fitting he'd be playing his last Big Ten game at the Metrodome.

"It's about 10 minutes from my home," he said. "The Iowa-Minnesota game up there in 1998 was my last start before I was injured for about three years. We got blown out [49-7]. It was a tough way to end the season, but it shows how far we've come now."

The 1998 Iowa-Minnesota game was Hayden Fry's last as the Hawkeyes' coach.

"The way we lost made it extra hard to see Hayden finish his career like that," Sobieski said. "I loved Coach Fry. He recruited me."

Sobieski underwent shoulder surgery following the 1998 season and took his redshirt year in 1999. Good idea. Iowa went 1-10 in a year that was Kirk Ferentz's first as the Hawkeyes' coach.

The 2000 season wasn't any bargain for Sobieski, either. He continued to be bothered by shoulder problems and again underwent surgery at midseason.

After being hampered by a groin injury early in the 2001 season, Sobieski played against Northwestern, Minnesota and Iowa State late in the year, but sat out the Alamo Bowl victory over Texas Tech.

He said he wasn't surprised that Ferentz had Iowa's program winning in a big-time way in 2002.

"I knew we had a lot of players, and I know we've got a very good coaching staff," Sobieski said.

Running off the Kinnick Stadium field one last time with the other senior offensive linemen in the Northwestern game was a thrill for Sobieski.

"That was the best thing I could ask for in my last home game," he said. "It gave every senior a chance to play in front of a great crowd. They told us we'd go out there for one play. We didn't plan on holding hands when we ran off. That decision was made at the last minute."

Banks 10 for 10 as a Passer

Iowa quarterback Brad Banks continued his 2002 magic against Northwestern by completing all 10 passes he attempted—throwing for 197 yards and three touchdowns in a 62-10 victory.

He also ran five times for 54 yards and two touchdowns, and Hawkeye fans were wondering if he was getting enough of a late-season push to make some noise in the Heisman Trophy race.

His 100 percent passing rate set a school record, and Coach Kirk Ferentz said after the game, "Brad's performance speaks volumes. You just have to look at what he does for our football team week in and week out.

"He's winning with his feet and his arm, but more importantly he's doing it with his head. He constantly puts us in good position, and the guys really believe in him."

Tears Before the Game

For Iowa senior defensive tackle Colin Cole, the tears started before his last home game in 2002.

"I felt tears coming to my eyes as I walked down the tunnel [toward the field]," Cole said after the Hawkeyes' 62-10 victory over Northwestern.

"It was hard to have only 60 minutes left in Kinnick Stadium.

"Coming in here, I thought I would be here a long time—an eternity. But, before you blink twice, it's your final season."

A Difference Between Being Hurt, Being Injured

As he prepared to start his 47th consecutive game for Iowa in its 2002 regular-season finale at Minnesota, center Bruce Nelson was asked if he ever came close to having the streak broken.

"I think if you're injured, you don't play," Nelson said. "If you're hurt, you play. I think we've all been hurt as football players. There's probably been a time when you've walked a fine line about whether you should be out there or not.

"I've been real fortunate in that I've never been injured. I've only been hurt. I've had a sore back, a deep thigh bruise—things like that."

Racism and Floyd of Rosedale

Since 1935, the team that has won the Iowa-Minnesota football game has been awarded the statue of a bronze pig named "Floyd of Rosedale."

Many people are not aware of it these days, but Floyd is the product of racism. So says former Iowa sports information director George Wine.

"I absolutely believe that," said Wine, who was the university's sports publicist for 25 years and has researched the Floyd of Rosedale situation.

"Ozzie Simmons was the star of Iowa's team, and he was one of very few blacks playing major college football at that time. For some reason, Minnesota played two consecutive games at Iowa, and won them both, when Simmons was on the team.

"Minnesota had manhandled Simmons while beating Iowa 48-12 in 1934. They were guilty of some late hits and abusive play against him. The next year the governor of Iowa, Clyde Herring, basically said he could not guarantee the safety of the Minnesota players because of what had happened to Simmons in 1934."

Wine said Floyd B. Olson, Minnesota's governor, tried to calm the situation by offering the bronze pig as the reward for winning the Iowa-Minnesota game. Olson made a bet with Herring on the 1935 game, with Floyd of Rosedale being the prize.

"Simmons said the 1935 game, which was won by Minnesota 13-6, was played cleanly and fairly," Wine said. "There were no racial incidents."

After Iowa lost, Herring presented Olson with Floyd, a full-blooded champion pig and a brother of BlueBoy from Will Rogers's movie *State Fair*.

Olson gave the pig to the University of Minnesota and commissioned St. Paul sculptor Charles Briescho to capture Floyd's image. The result was a bronze pig 21 inches long and 15 inches high.

Minnesota holds a 38-28-2 advantage in the series since Floyd of Rosedale has been on the line, but Iowa has won the last two games—including a 45-21 victory in 2002.

Going into that game, Iowa center Bruce Nelson said,

"I think Floyd likes this corn-fed stuff. So we'll try to keep him around."

At Eight, Banks Did the "Heisman Pose"

With Iowa quarterback Brad Banks receiving some Heisman Trophy mention late in the 2002 season, the story got out that the senior from Belle Glade, Florida, knew more about the award than he had let on earlier.

It turned out that Banks even knew something about the "Heisman pose."

"I was eight years of age when I first did the pose," Banks said. "We'd run around the neighborhood when we were kids and do the pose when we scored a touch-down."

Banks then said he had brushed up on his Iowa football history by taking a look at Floyd of Rosedale, the bronze pig that's awarded to the winner of the Iowa-Minnesota game every season.

"Was he doing the Heisman pose?" I asked.

"No, he wasn't doing the pose," Banks said.

And, speaking of the Heisman pose, Banks wouldn't take a reporter up on his request to have the quarterback do the pose.

"My leg is stiff," he said with a laugh and not sounding very truthful.

Clark Dedicated Games to His Late Mother

Iowa tight end Dallas Clark said his father, Doug, of Livermore, Iowa, and his older brother, Derrik, a former Iowa State player now living in Des Moines, would be among family members attending the 2002 Iowa-Minnesota game at Minneapolis.

And his mother?

"She passed away five days before I graduated from high school in 1998," Clark explained. "She had a heart attack at 49.

"Her name was Jan, and I dedicate every game I play to her. She and my dad were divorced, and I lived with her."

This Was One for the Ages

I've witnessed some big-time victories by Iowa football teams over the more than half-century I've watched them play, but none any more exciting than the one at Minnesota on November 16, 2002.

On a day when the Hawkeyes needed to win to secure a school-record 11th regular-season victory and 8-0 Big Ten Conference season, they pulled it off brilliantly.

"It's going to be hard to knock a smile off my face for a while," Coach Kirk Ferentz said after his team blitzed Minnesota 45-21 in front of 65,184 fans at the Metrodome—at least half of whom were cheering for Iowa.

Long-stemmed roses were all over the place—including in the right hand of Ferentz as he was carried off the field by his jubilant players. The roses, of course, were indicative that Iowa's fans and players were expecting the team to play in the Rose Bowl on January 1, 2003.

Who cared if Ferentz and his players would be headed to Miami, Florida, and the Orange Bowl instead of the Rose Bowl in Pasadena, California?

"I have no idea what's going to happen, and I don't care," Ferentz said moments after the Hawkeyes finished their regular-season schedule. "All I wanted us to do was win this game today."

Even though Iowa played so brilliantly in the Big Ten season, it had to share the conference title with Ohio State, which improved its record to 8-0 a week later while the Hawkeyes were idle.

After Iowa's victory in Minneapolis and before Ferentz stepped behind the postgame microphones in a crowded downstairs hallway at the Metrodome, I stood on the field near the Iowa bench, near Floyd of Rosedale—the trophy that's awarded annually to the Iowa-Minnesota winner—near the excited Hawkeye players, near the Iowa marching band that had the made the trip north for this important game.

It was a scene for the ages.

I couldn't help but feel good for Ferentz, whose future as Iowa's coach was certainly put in doubt with the 1-10 and 3-9 records he had in his first two seasons.

I also felt good for Bob Bowlsby, the athletic director who had been criticized so heavily for choosing Ferentz over fan favorite Bob Stoops after Hayden Fry retired in 1998.

But, more than anything, I felt good for Iowa's fans. Those people who live in Iowa City, Des Moines, Cedar Rapids, Lone Tree, Morning Sun, Montezuma, Victor and all the other cities and small towns in Iowa are from a low-population state that far too often seems to be on the outside looking in when the Michigans and Ohio States of the Big Ten football world are winning championships.

This was Iowa's day to celebrate, just as it was on November 21, 1981 when Fry's team sewed up a Rose Bowl berth by routing Michigan State 36-7; just as it was on November 17, 1956 when Forest Evashevski's team won the Big Ten title with 60 minutes of unbelievable defense that produced a 6-0 victory over Woody Hayes and his Ohio State squad.

I was there for those games, too. But this one on November 16, 2002—played in an indoor arena against a team that has, for many years, been a bitter rival of Iowa—was certainly as impressive.

"Believe me, nobody has enjoyed this year as much as I have," Ferentz said.

Banks Voted Player of the Year

It wasn't the Heisman Trophy, but it wasn't exactly a kick in the pants, either.

Iowa quarterback Brad Banks continued his unbelievable ride through college football's magic kingdom when he was named the College Player of the Year by the Associated Press.

Not bad for a guy who had never started a collegiate game until his senior season at Iowa.

Not bad for a guy who was a backup to Kyle McCann, the Hawkeye quarterback who was booed by his own fans in his own stadium in 2001.

Not bad for a guy who, before the 2002 season began, said very few people recognized him as Iowa's quarterback when they saw him walking through the campus.

"I can't imagine a better success story," Iowa coach Kirk Ferentz said after learning that Banks had won the AP award. "Brad wasn't on anybody's radar screen in late-August. But he improved every week, and played his best in our biggest games."

Banks was already preparing for Iowa's Orange Bowl game against Southern California. In the AP balloting, he edged USC Carson Palmer by three votes.

"I'm kind of shocked to hear I've won this," Banks said of the AP award. "I'm very happy the way the season went, and the way everyone on this team made Iowa a household name. I'm glad to play a part in all this."

Banks added, "With the number of great players in college football, this is truly a humbling experience. I became what I am because of over 100 other players on the Iowa roster and a great coaching staff.

"My teammates made me a better player, and hopefully, I helped make them better players along the way."

Iowa's Fourth Heisman Runner-up

Quarterback Brad Banks became the fourth Iowa player to finish second in voting for the Heisman Trophy on December 14, 2002.

The previous runners-up were Alex Karras in 1957, Randy Duncan in 1958 and Chuck Long in 1985. Iowa's only Heisman winner was Nile Kinnick, the standout halfback on Coach Eddie Anderson's 1939 Ironmen.

Banks, who was named the Associated Press College Football Player of the Year and won the Davey O'Brien Award that goes to the nation's best quarterback, was beaten out by another quarterback for the Heisman.

The winner was Carson Palmer of Southern California, who would play against Iowa in the Orange Bowl in Miami less than three weeks later.

Barr Questioned Bowl Opponent

With the Orange Bowl getting closer, outspoken Iowa linebacker Fred Barr questioned whether USC was physical enough to handle Iowa in the game.

"They're a good team with very talented people, but they're missing the physical aspect which we're bringing to the game," Barr said. "You still have to play between the lines.

"Playing in the Big Ten every week, we pound it week in and week out. I don't think they play that kind of football in the Pac-10."

Barr also wasn't all that thrilled that USC's Carson Palmer beat out Hawkeye teammate Brad Banks for the Heisman Trophy.

"I thought Brad was going to win," Barr said. "He did a lot more for our team than Carson did for his team. I think Brad should have won it."

Asked if the fact that Palmer, the Heisman winner, would be Iowa's opponent might provide the Hawkeyes with extra motivation, Barr said, "I think the motivation will be that we beat a lot of teams this year, but we're still not getting the respect we need to get right now."

Game Plan: "Pound 'Em"

Pound 'em.

That's what Fred Russell had in mind. And maybe his coaches had the same thing in mind.

Iowa's Orange Bowl game was still a few days away when Russell kept talking about pounding away at Southern California's defense.

"Hopefully, we can wear them down with a good offensive line and the good backs we have," said Russell.

Russell was certainly one of those good backs. He was good enough to be named a first-team all-Big Ten player.

Russell, a junior running back who missed two games because of injuries, led the Hawkeyes with 1,219 yards during the regular season. Jermelle Lewis, his main backup, totaled 678.

Asked his thoughts on Iowa being a one-touchdown underdog to USC, Russell said, "We've been the underdogs all year. That's nothing new to us."

"Lots of Pretty Girls"

Iowa linebacker Fred Barr said it wasn't the players from Florida that Coach Kirk Ferentz had to worry about when the Hawkeyes arrived in Miami for the Orange Bowl.

"I think Ferentz will have to worry more about the Iowa guys," Barr said. "They won't know the atmosphere down there."

And what would the players—whether they were from Florida, Iowa or anywhere else—find when they arrived?

"Lots of pretty girls," Barr answered. "It will be fun."

Oh, sure. It figured there would be plenty of opportunity for the Hawkeyes to have fun in Miami. That's the case at any bowl site. But Ferentz planned to make sure there were limits put on the fun as Iowa's journey south got closer.

"This game isn't [a matter] of life and death," Ferentz said.

"But we want to go down there and win the thing, and it's going to take our best effort. To win a 12th game this season would be special and significant.

"We'd wind up being ranked second or third in the country. That's uncharted territory for us [in recent history]. But, if it doesn't work out, it's not going to diminish what's been a great season already."

Asked about the 12 Florida players on his team, Ferentz said, "Those are the guys I've got to watch" in the pre-Orange Bowl activities. "They've all got friends down there. That's the one bad thing about not going to the West Coast [for the Rose Bowl].

"We have only three guys from California, and it's easier to keep track of those guys. The Florida guys might be a bigger challenge.

"But, again, you're talking about guys like Fred Barr and Colin Cole. They're playing their last ballgame. They don't want to go down there and lay an egg, I can assure you of that. I can't say enough about this team and how they've handled themselves.

"Quite frankly, the guys I worry about on bowl trips are the freshmen—the guys who know they're not going to play. They don't worry about being at full strength. They're the guys we'll keep honest."

Half of the 12 Florida players on Iowa's roster were from Fort Lauderdale. They included Barr, Cole, wide receiver Mo Brown, defensive tackle Fabian Dodd, linebacker Abdul Hodge and linebacker George Lewis.

Other Floridians were quarterback Brad Banks of Belle Glade, wide receiver C. J. Jones of Boynton Beach, linebacker Edmond Miles of Tallahassee, defense back Marcus Paschal of Largo, defensive lineman Larry Thomas of Miami and defensive back Antwan Allen of Tampa.

Raising the Barr

More from Fred Barr, Iowa's talkative linebacker, before the 2003 Orange Bowl:

"The Alamo Bowl [where Iowa beat Texas Tech 19-16 in 2001] was all right. It was a good little bowl. But it definitely wasn't the Orange Bowl [where the Hawkeyes would later lose to Southern California].

"I considered leaving Iowa early in my career, but every kid goes through that. The weather is so cold in Iowa. I'm not used to wearing a jacket every day. It's a change, but you can get used to it.

"The guys from Florida on this team are a tight-knit group." How about losing Benny Sapp, the cornerback who was kicked off the team by Ferentz in August 2002, and transferred to Northern Iowa? "He comes down to Iowa City every once in a while and we still hang out. We're still tight.

"Coach [Kirk] Ferentz sometimes cries after a big win."

Orange Bowl Turns Sour

Although an enormous number of Iowa fans turned Pro Player Stadium in Miami into "Kinnick Stadium South," Southern California ruined the Hawkeyes' first trip to the Orange Bowl on January 2, 2003. After a 10-10 halftime tie, USC stormed to a 38-17 victory in a game that attracted a sellout crowd of 75,971 fans—an estimated 50,000 of whom were cheering for Iowa.

But the huge Hawkeye throng could do nothing to stop Carson Palmer, the USC quarterback who earlier beat out Iowa's Brad Banks for the Heisman Trophy.

And the Iowa fans could do nothing to help an Iowa offense that, uncharacteristically, was unable to do anything to pierce USC's defense. Without a doubt, the Hawkeyes were overmatched by a talented, quicker team.

"It's been 28 games since we lost a game like this," Iowa coach Kirk Ferentz said, showing that he was well schooled on recent Hawkeye football history.

Ferentz was referring to a 38-10 regular-season loss to Ohio State on October 21, 2000.

Palmer completed 21 of 31 passes for 303 yards and one touchdown against an Iowa team that, at the time, was ranked No. 3 nationally. Before the game, some of the Hawkeyes' players had questioned whether Palmer deserved to be the Heisman Trophy winner ahead of Banks.

But not afterward.

"He definitely proved his point," Hawkeye line-backer Fred Barr said of Palmer. "He's a good quarter-back and I can't take anything away from him."

However, Barr said Iowa's defense "was on the field too long. We were keying on passes thrown by the Heisman Trophy winner, and USC ran the ball down our throats."

Iowa had been giving up an average of only 68.2 yards per game on the ground, but USC ran for 247.

"Embarrassing," Says Brad Banks

Iowa quarterback Brad Banks, who led the nation in passing efficiency and threw only four interceptions during the regular season, had his first pass in 101 attempts picked off in the fourth quarter of the Orange Bowl game.

"It's embarrassing," Banks said after the game. "It's tough to lose a game like this."

Iowa had been a fast-starting team all season and gave its fans reason to think the Orange Bowl would be a continuation of what happened in its march to an 8-0 Big Ten record.

C. J. Jones, the Hawkeyes' senior wide receiver from Boynton Beach, Florida, and a cousin of Banks, put a charge into everyone in the stadium by returning the opening kickoff 100 yards for a touchdown.

It marked the third 100-yard return of an opening kickoff for a touchdown in Iowa football history, and it was the longest opening kickoff return ever in an Orange Bowl game.

"I never thought I'd set a record in the Orange Bowl," Jones said. "I probably knew I was gone for the touchdown at about the 50-yard line. I had Jermelle Lewis in front of me, and I kind of pushed him in the back so he'd stay there.

"This was my biggest thrill ever as a football player. I had quite a few members of my family, plus friends, here for the game, so it was a great feeling to run the kickoff back in front of them."

"Outplayed in Every Phase"

Iowa Coach Kirk Ferentz said he "felt good about our chances" at halftime of the Orange Bowl game when the score was 10-10.

"But we did some things to hurt ourselves," he commented. "USC totally dominated the second half. They outplayed us in every phase."

Iowa was penalized a season-high 13 times in the game, and Ferentz was asked if those mistakes and the problems Banks had were the result of Iowa being rusty from having not played a game since November 16.

"I'm not sure," Ferentz said. "We had more than our share of penalties in the first half, and Brad wasn't throwing the ball sharply. I had some concerns seven or eight days ago [about the team being ready for the Orange Bowl], but left the practice field two days ago feeling pretty good.

"We thought we had our bases covered, but obviously we didn't."

Last Game or First Game?

Of Iowa's Orange Bowl loss to Southern California, standout Hawkeye offensive guard Eric Steinbach said, "We don't like to make excuses, but we played like it was our first game of the season instead of the last.

"It's tough to wind up the season this way. We'd like to go out as champions on top. But it just didn't work out that way.

"But, after a couple of days when we're able to put this game behind us, we'll remember that we're Big Ten champions. There will be a time when we sit back and look at the positives."

Steinbach said there's a bright football future at Iowa.

"Coach Ferentz and his staff are doing a tremendous job," he said. "This team will be going to bowl games from here on out."

Layoff Was Too Long

Ed Podolak, a standout Iowa back in the 1960s who went on to star for the Kansas City Chiefs, has played in and seen enough big football games to draw some clear-cut conclusions.

Podolak, who in 2002 was in his 21st year as an analyst on radio broadcasts of Hawkeye games, figured he knew what the team's problems were against Southern California in the Orange Bowl.

"There's no way you can take a layoff that long and expect to play well," Podolak said of the 47 days between Iowa's regular-season finale and the Orange Bowl. "USC's layoff was three weeks shorter, and it showed in conditioning and in the way Brad Banks played quarterback for Iowa.

"Banks had been flying all over the country and just wasn't in synch at the Orange Bowl.

"I still think Iowa and USC were pretty evenly matched, and that was evident at halftime," Podolak said. "But Iowa just ran out of gas. You can get in shape, but you can't get in game shape without playing. Plus, that kid at quarterback for USC [Carson Palmer] had a world-class game."

The Orange Bowl loss ended any hope the 2002 Hawkeyes had of being named the best Iowa team ever.

But Chuck Hartlieb, a standout Iowa quarterback who lettered from 1986-1988, said even a victory over Southern California wouldn't have given the 2002 team the "best" label.

"I don't think the best-ever team would have lost to Iowa State the way that one did," Hartlieb explained.

Iowa Finishes No. 8 in Rankings

Iowa slid from No. 3 to No. 8 in both the final Associated Press and coaches' polls following the loss to Southern California in the Orange Bowl.

Still, the No. 3 ranking was the highest for a Hawkeye team since Coach Forest Evashevski's 1960 team had an 8-1 record and finished No. 2 in the United Press International poll and No. 3 in the Associated Press poll.

EDDIE PODOLAK

"Most Complete Team"

Jim Zabel, the longtime announcer for WHO in Des Moines, was in the radio booth for broadcasts of games coached by nine Iowa coaches—Eddie Anderson, Leonard Raffensperger, Forest Evashevski, Jerry Burns, Ray Nagel, Frank Lauterbur, Bob Commings, Hayden Fry and Kirk Ferentz.

"The last five years of Evashevski and the first 10 years of Fry were the best," Zabel said.

I asked Zabel how he felt Kirk Ferentz's 2002 squad would rank with Evashevski's great teams.

"You're almost comparing apples and oranges," he said. "But Ferentz's 2002 team was maybe the most complete team overall. They had a great kicking game, great offense, good defense and good special teams."

Clark's Collegiate Career Ends

Dallas Clark's Iowa football career wound up shorter than expected.

The 6'4", 244-pound tight end, who came to school without a football scholarship, said on January 16, 2003— two weeks after the Orange Bowl game—that he had decided to pass up his final season of eligibility to make himself available for the National Football League draft.

It was hard to argue against Clark's decision. I sure couldn't.

He was older than most college juniors. He turned 24 on June 12, 2003, and said he felt giving the NFL a shot was the right thing for him to do at this stage in his life.

Clark couldn't have asked for a better final collegiate season. He was named winner of the John Mackey Award that goes to the nation's best tight end; he was a Walter Camp Foundation first-team All-American; first-team Associated Press All-American; first-team Football Writers Association of America All-American; first-team *Sporting News* All-American and All-Big Ten player; first-team CNNSI.com All-American; first-team ESPN.com All-American, and first-team All-Big Ten.

Clark, from the small Iowa community of Livermore, was quite a success story. He became the nation's premier collegiate tight end in 2002 after being switched from reserve linebacker in the spring of 2001.

He was Iowa's second leading receiver during the regular season with 39 catches for 645 yards and four touchdowns. He caught four more passes for 97 yards in the Orange Bowl.

But Ferentz Decides to Stay at Iowa

You know it. I know it.

A coach wins. Another team tries to hire him. It happens all the time.

But Kirk Ferentz stepped up to say no.

This very important guy in the Iowa football picture didn't head to the National Football League after the magical 2002 season.

Still, Ferentz, who had scoffed at any suggestion that he might leave Iowa for an NFL job following the season, kept Hawkeye fans in a state of nervousness after interviewing with the Jacksonville Jaguars.

But he was never offered the job. And, in mid-January 2003, Ferentz said he was staying at Iowa.

"The attention I have received regarding the Jacksonville Jaguars has been flattering, especially because I have the utmost regard for Wayne Weaver [the club's owner] and the entire Jacksonville organization," Ferentz said.

"However, my heart continues to be with the University of Iowa, and I will remain the head coach of the Hawkeye football team."

Iowa even sweetened the pot to make Ferentz's decision to stay easier.

Ferentz was given an eight percent pay raise of $72,800. The bump in pay pushed his salary to $982,800. However, with incentive bonuses, his pay was much more than that.

Chapter 2
Nile Kinnick's 1939 Ironmen

Depression, Then Big-Time Success

It was 1939, and agricultural Iowa still hadn't completely recovered from the Great Depression.

Certainly, football at the University of Iowa was still depressed.

The Hawkeyes were coming off 1-7 and 1-6-1 records under teams coached by Irl Tubbs in 1937 and 1938. With little to look forward to on the football field, fans stayed away from the stadium on Saturdays.

"In those days, they had nothing to cheer about," said Erwin Prasse, now of Naperville, Illinois.

Prasse was an end on the football team and one of the best athletes the university ever produced.

"It was the stupid Depression, and it hurt the farmers especially," Prasse said. "The state was really down."

But it turned out there was some light at the end of the tunnel.

Actually, a number of lights.

One was named Dr. Eddie Anderson. Another was Nile Kinnick. Another was Al Couppee. And, yes, certainly another was Erwin Prasse himself.

It was 1939. It was the year of the famous Ironmen.

Dr. Eddie Anderson's Arrival

Eddie Anderson was a native Iowan. He was born in Oskaloosa and attended high school in Mason City.

He had been an All-America football player at Notre Dame, where his coach was the legendary Knute Rockne.

Indeed, Anderson was a member of the Notre Dame team in 1921 that came to Iowa City with a 20-game winning streak. But the Hawkeyes jolted the Fighting Irish 10-7, in the first of their two consecutive unbeaten seasons under Coach Howard Jones.

Anderson, an ambitious young man, studied at Rush Medical College and became a physician—specializing in urology. But he still wanted to be a football coach.

So he became the head coach at Holy Cross, where he had a 47-7-2 record from 1933-1938.

Obviously, for a university looking for a promising coach, Anderson was someone to keep an eye on.

That's exactly what Iowa officials did after Coach Irl Tubbs's 1938 team had a 1-6-1 record in 1938.

"The only team we beat was the University of Chicago, and then they soon dropped out of the Big Ten," standout Hawkeye end Erwin Prasse said.

"Ernie Nevers was then one of our assistant coaches. When he heard about Chicago leaving the conference, he said, 'Gee, there goes our winning streak!'"

Losses to Minnesota, Indiana and Nebraska ended Tubbs's days as Iowa's coach, and Iowa went after Anderson.

Smart move.

The Coaching Doctor

As far as I'm concerned, the most amazing thing about Dr. Eddie Anderson when he was coaching Iowa's football team was that he also practiced medicine.

Can you imagine one of today's major college coaches practicing urology at a hospital until early in the afternoon, then running football practices until late in the day?

Not me.

"Anderson did his medical work at the hospital in the mornings, then he'd be wearing his doctor's clothes when he showed up at the practice field," said George "Red" Frye, who was a center on Anderson's 1939 team. "He then would change into his football clothes."

End Erwin Prasse said, "The hospital wasn't too far from the practice field. Anderson would stay at the hospital until about 2 p.m., then come to the practice field."

Frye said Anderson, despite his medical training, had a simple remedy for curing a sore ankle on a player.

"He'd say, 'Run it off!' if he saw someone limping," Frye said. "He didn't want anyone limping around. He had no sympathy for you."

COACH EDDIE ANDERSON WITH 1939 BACKFIELD

Heisman Trophy Winner,
But Not Captain

The Main Man of the 1939 Iowa Ironmen was Nile Kinnick, the do-everything halfback who went on to become Iowa's only Heisman Trophy winner.

Kinnick, whose grandfather—George W. Clarke—had been governor of the State of Iowa from 1913-1917, was an extremely intelligent young man who appeared destined for big things after his days as a Hawkeye star.

Could he have been elected governor? A Senator? To an even higher office?

Unfortunately, we'll never know.

Tragically, Kinnick's life ended on June 2, 1943. As a navy ensign, he died when his plane crashed on a training flight in the Caribbean Sea. He was only 24.

Kinnick grew up in Adel, Iowa, a town just west of Des Moines, but spent his senior year in high school in Omaha, Nebraska. He and his teammates had been part of just two victories and one tie in 16 Iowa games under Coach Irl Tubbs in 1937 and 1938.

Kinnick wasn't elected captain of the 1939 team. Instead, Prasse was.

"Kinnick had counted on being captain, and I thought he certainly would be," said Prasse, who went on to earn nine letters in football, basketball and baseball at Iowa. "But he had a bad ankle in 1938, and I was named our most valuable player.

"Looking back now, what the hell difference did it make that I was the captain in 1939? The captain decides what you're going to do when the officials flip the coin, and that's it."

Even though Kinnick wasn't the team's captain, he was just about everything else on the campus in 1939.

In addition to winning the Heisman Trophy—the award that goes to the most outstanding collegiate player in the nation—he was named America's Athlete of the Year over such professional standouts as boxer Joe Louis and the New York Yankees' Joe DiMaggio.

Kinnick also was awarded football's Maxwell Award (nation's best all-around player), the Walter Camp Award (nation's top player), led the balloting for the College All-Star game and was named the Big Ten's most valuable player.

If that wasn't enough, he was a Phi Beta Kappa scholar and was president of his senior class at Iowa. He earned a 3.4 grade point average in Iowa's College of Commerce and was enrolled in the College of Law before entering military service.

In 1972—29 years after Kinnick's death in the crash of his navy fighter plane in the Caribbean Sea—the name of Iowa Stadium was changed to Kinnick Stadium in his honor.

Good Friend Jim Hoak Recalls Kinnick

Jim Hoak, who grew up in Des Moines, was perhaps Nile Kinnick's best friend at the University of Iowa.

"Nile was from Adel, Iowa, and I attended Roosevelt High School in Des Moines," Hoak told me when he was 84 years of age. "One summer we were playing Junior Legion baseball, even though I wasn't much of a player.

"We played a game against Van Meter, and Bob Feller pitched for them. Kinnick was the Van Meter catcher. Nile Kinnick Sr. and my dad were friends, and when I was ready to play that baseball game, my dad said, 'You know, there's a kid from Adel on that Van Meter team whose dad I know real well. Say hello to him.'

"From that time on, Nile and I were together a lot. He'd come to Des Moines and we became good friends."

The Bob Feller who pitched for Van Meter, of course, went on to become a major-league Hall of Fame player for the Cleveland Indians.

"Kinnick came to the University of Iowa at the same time I did in the fall of 1936," Hoak said. "He lived in the Quadrangle dormitory for one year. At the start of his second year, he moved into the Phi Kappa Psi fraternity.

"I was already living there, and Nile and I became roommates until we graduated in June, 1940. I had been president of the fraternity, and Nile was our finance man.

"I played on the Iowa golf team for three years and was captain of the squad for one year. I played on the freshman football team with Nile, and I also was on the freshman basketball team with him."

In addition to lettering in football in 1937, 1938 and 1939, Kinnick lettered in basketball in 1938.

Kinnick's Stirring Heisman Speech

Heisman Trophy winner Nile Kinnick of Iowa clearly demonstrated his extraordinary public speaking skills when he was given the 1939 award in New York City.

I haven't heard every Heisman speech that's been given, but I've listened to a number of them. I can't help but believe that there has ever been a more stirring speech at the Heisman ceremony.

With the United States soon to be at war, here's what Kinnick said:

"Thank you very, very kindly, Mr. Holcomb. It seems to me that everyone is letting their superlatives run away with them this evening, but nonetheless, I want you to know that I'm mighty, mighty happy to accept this trophy this evening.

"Every football player in these United States dreams about winning that trophy and of this fine trip to New York. Every player considers that trophy the acme in recognition of this kind. And the fact that I am actually receiving this trophy tonight almost overwhelms me, and I know that all of those boys who have gone before me must have felt somewhat the same way.

"From my own personal viewpoint, I consider my winning this award as indirectly, a great tribute to the coaching staff at the University of Iowa, headed by Dr. Eddie Anderson, and to my teammates sitting back in Iowa City. A finer man and a better coach never hit these United States, and a finer bunch of boys never graced the gridirons of the Midwest than that Iowa team in 1939. I wish that they might all be with me tonight to receive this trophy. They certainly deserve it.

"I want to take this grand opportunity to thank collectively, all the sportswriters and all the sportscasters, and all those who have seen fit, have seen their way clear to cast a ballot in my favor for this trophy. And I also want to take this opportunity to thank Mr. Prince and his committee, the Heisman Award committee, and all those connected with the Downtown Athletic Club for this trophy, and for the fine time that they're showing me. And not only for that, but for making this fine and worthy trophy available to the football players of the country.

"Finally, if you will permit me, I'd like to make a comment which in my mind is indicative, perhaps, of the greater significance of football, and sports emphasis in general in this country, and that is, I thank God I was warring on the gridirons of the Midwest and not on the battlefields of Europe. I can speak confidently and positively that the players of this country would much more, much rather struggle and fight to win the Heisman award than the Croix de Guerre.

"Thank you."

"Get the Kid to the Dinner on Time"

Jim Hoak, who had watched his good friend, Nile Kinnick, play in all eight of Iowa's football games in the magical 1939 season, also went to New York City with him for the Heisman Trophy ceremony.

"Dr. Eddie Anderson, the coach, called me one evening and told me Nile was a Heisman finalist," Hoak explained. "Later, he called to say Nile had won the Heisman, and he needed somebody to go with him to New York.

"So Eddie made arrangements for Nile and I to go. Eddie, of course, also went. We all took the train from Iowa City to Chicago, then caught a plane from there to New York.

"We arrived on Friday, and the Heisman Trophy was to be presented on Saturday night. I'll never forget what Eddie told me on Friday. He said, 'Now just one thing, Jim. Get the kid to the dinner on time.' That was my job."

Kinnick, Hoak Saw the Sights

Jim Hoak said he and Nile Kinnick did all the things tourists were supposed to do when they arrived in New York City for the Heisman Trophy ceremony.

"I had been to New York a few times, but I don't think Nile had ever been there," Hoak said. "I had some friends there, so we were out and saw the bright spots. We did all the rubberneck things kids would do there.

"We saw the Statue of Liberty, the Empire State Building and other things. In fact, we went to the top of the Empire State Building."

How Kinnick Fashioned That Great Speech

During the trip to New York City, Nile Kinnick made this comment to his friend, Jim Hoak: "You know, I suppose they'll call on me to say something."

Kinnick was referring to the fact that he'd be called on to give a speech after receiving the Heisman Trophy.

"I said, 'Nile, they always do. You're going to be the honoree. You'd better at least have some thoughts.'"

Hoak then described to me how Kinnick went into action.

"On the back of his airline ticket he scratched out his idea that he'd rather win the Heisman than go to the Croix de Guerre," Hoak explained.

Kinnick looked at Hoak and said, "What do you think?"

"That sounds all right to me," Hoak answered.

More than 60 years later, Hoak told me, "Nile and I knew that war may be coming. We weren't there yet, but we thought we were going to be involved in a war in some manner.

"But that's all Nile wrote in preparation for giving the speech—the squib saying he'd rather win the Heisman than go to the Croix de Guerre. He put the whole thing together in his head."

Hoak said all Kinnick carried with him when he went to the microphone to give his acceptance speech was "a piece of paper no bigger than a business card. He really had no formal speech prepared. He spoke extemporaneously, and I promise you that neither Eddie Anderson nor I nor anyone else had anything to do with it."

Hoak sat in the back of the room while Kinnick spoke. The brilliant speech didn't surprise Hoak.

"Nile was always very good on his feet, and he had a wonderful command of the language," Hoak said. "Although he was shy, he always liked speaking."

Hoak said the speech Kinnick made was "typical Nile."

When Hoak and Kinnick talked to one another at the end of the evening, Kinnick said, "Do you think I did all right?"

"You did very well. You did excellent," Hoak told the Heisman Trophy winner.

After that exchange, Kinnick asked Hoak if they were supposed to see Dr. Eddie Anderson any more that night.

"No, Eddie will see us at the airplane tomorrow morning," Hoak said.

Stadium Named in Kinnick's Honor

In 1972, Iowa Stadium was renamed Kinnick Stadium in honor of Heisman Trophy winner Nile Kinnick.

Construction of the stadium was completed October 5, 1929 at a cost of $497,151.42. The original capacity was 53,000. The present capacity is 70,397.

Kinnick "No Goody Two-Shoes"

Nile Kinnick's personality has remained somewhat of a mystery over the years.

No one outside his immediate family knew him any better than Jim Hoak, who was his friend before and during the years at the University of Iowa.

"He was no Goody Two-Shoes, I'll tell you that," Hoak said. "Not only were we fraternity roommates at Iowa, he lived with me two summers and we worked together.

"Nile had fun and he liked the girls. He had a couple of girlfriends, though not serious ones. He enjoyed going to dances, but he wasn't the type of gregarious guy who would go out and chase girls.

"We'd go to some of the little taverns around school, and he'd have an occasional drink—but not more than one. On New Year's Eve or something like that, he'd have fun, have a drink and make a little noise. He was not one to go to the taverns in Iowa City by himself. He'd go with three or four of us, and maybe he'd have a date."

Hoak said Kinnick was "very shy around everybody until he got to know them. Once he knew people, he loved to express his opinions.

"He was always kind of a leader in a group of young men at an organization or in a fraternity house. You could see he was very bright. He always kept up to date on what was going on in the world. He knew the names of foreign dignitaries, heads of state and generals that the rest of us would pass over as not being very important."

And his memory? Outstanding.

"He had a great memory," Hoak said. "He could remember everything."

What Might Have Been

Because of Nile Kinnick's intelligence, his training in law school and his ability to lead, many imagined him as someone with a strong political future.

Don't forget, his grandfather, George W. Clarke, had been an Iowa governor.

"Nile was very politically minded," said his friend, Jim Hoak. "The New Deal was in high gear at the time, and he was very quick to point out the shortcomings of people getting things without deserving them. He was critical of that. He thought people should make their own way.

"He was not what I'd call raving right wing, but he was a Republican in his thoughts. He could well have become a governor, a United States Senator or something. Who knows? He would probably have gone into politics. He talked about it all the time, with his law degree and his ability to get up and express himself.

"He'd have been a formidable political candidate. Although he did get his law degree, he never took the bar exam. He really wasn't that anxious to enlist in the military, but there was so much pressure on him. He was kind of pushed into it."

Kinnick, Anderson a Perfect Match

The timing was perfect for Nile Kinnick and Eddie Anderson in 1939.

Anderson, who was in his first season as Iowa's coach, needed Kinnick as much as Nile, who was in his final season as a Hawkeye player, needed Anderson.

The result was Anderson's 6-1-1 season, which was his best in his eight years as Iowa's coach.

"Nile liked Eddie Anderson," said Jim Hoak, Kinnick's friend. "He did think Eddie was a little coarse. He'd always laugh at some of the jokes Eddie told because Eddie was very profane.

"Nile used very little profanity. He was never vulgar. He'd delete any vulgar words that were part of a story.

"But Nile wouldn't have gotten to where he was without a good coach, and Eddie happened to be the right one. No question about that. Iowa was not a great team in 1938 (when the record was 1-6-1 under Irl Tubbs's coaching), but that all changed in 1939."

Bill Reichardt, a nine-year-old mascot on the 1939 team and later the most valuable player in the Big Ten as an Iowa fullback in 1951, says, "Kinnick was the perfect kind of player for Anderson. He was always well-dressed, his hair was always neat and he was very bright. Anderson almost took him on as a son."

Kinnick and Christian Science

Nile Kinnick's Christian Science beliefs have been talked about for many years.

Indeed, some people still say that Kinnick almost decided not to play for first-year coach Eddie Anderson, a Catholic, in his senior season because of differing religious philosophies.

"I can guarantee you that is totally false," Jim Hoak, Kinnick's friend and fraternity roommate, told me.

"At first, Nile was a little skeptical of anyone coming in. But when Eddie was announced as the head coach, Nile checked to see who he was and was thrilled to death that he'd be playing for him."

Some people have also said that Kinnick wouldn't agree to have injuries treated by physicians because of Christian Science beliefs.

Not true, said Hoak.

"Nile's mother was a Christian Scientist, but his father was kind of halfway—like Nile," Hoak said. "Nile didn't attend church in Iowa City. If he listed a church affiliation, I'm sure he would have said Christian Science, but he was not a religious nut of any kind."

Erwin Prasse, Kinnick's teammate at Iowa, said Nile would even wrap his own ankles before practice and games because of his beliefs.

"Nile had a bad ankle the entire 1938 season," Prasse said. "Because he was a Christian Scientist, he taped his own ankles. He didn't want anyone else fooling with him."

That wasn't the full explanation, Hoak commented.

"He wrapped his own ankles," Hoak said, "but not because of any Christian Science beliefs. He had been taught to wrap his ankles a certain way—in figure-eight manner—by some guy in Omaha, and he wanted to do it that way.

"But he went to doctors when there was something wrong with him."

Kinnick, the Drop-Kicker

George "Red" Frye of Albia, Iowa, who was a sophomore center on the 1939 team, spent considerable time on the practice field with Nile Kinnick.

"Nile was among the last of the drop-kickers, and we'd go out and work on that," Frye explained. "We'd also have someone retrieve the ball after Nile kicked it.

"Nile would start on the right side of the 20-yard line on the practice field. I'd center him the ball and he'd drop-kick it at that angle. Then he'd take a step to the left until he got to the other side of the field. We'd go out there almost every night."

Prasse, Frye Recall Kinnick

Erwin Prasse, left end and captain of Iowa's 1939 Ironmen, was 85 years of age and living in Naperville, Illinois, when he recalled Nile Kinnick as "a fine gentleman and a very, very smart person.

"I certainly believe he deserved the Heisman Trophy. Nobody could come close to him in those days. If he didn't get it, there would have been a riot in the state of Iowa."

Iowa center George "Red" Frye, 84, said he "knew Kinnick as well as anybody, although he wasn't that close to anybody. He kind of stood his distance. He wasn't 'stuck up' or anything—he'd talk to anybody. He was an individualist and a perfectionist."

Prasse, like Frye, remembered Kinnick as someone who kept his distance from others on the football team.

"He was always studying," Prasse said. "Dick 'Whitey' Evans, the starting right end, and I were typical jocks—even though I think I was a little brighter than Whitey.

"Whitey and I were in the same geology class with Kinnick. Nile lived in a dormitory near Iowa Fieldhouse, and Whitey and I would go over to his room. Nile would tell us what to study.

"He'd have his textbook there and he had a knack of knowing what the questions would be from the professor."

Prasse had an explanation for that.

"Kinnick had a lot more attention given to him as a student when he was young," Prasse explained. "My dad [whose first name was also Erwin] worked nights all the time. The only time I saw him was at suppertime.

"He was from the old country—Germany. Pa was the kindest person and the most loving person, but he spent no time with me. He was in the bakery business. In fact, the only football game he saw me play was our last one in 1939 at Northwestern—my finale for Iowa.

"My mother told Pa that if he didn't go that game she was going to kill him. After the game [a 7-7 tie], I took my shower and came out to see Pa. I said, 'Pa, what do you think of American football?' He said, 'A-h-h-h.'"

In other words, Pa wasn't all that excited about what the Ironmen or any other collegiate football team did in the United States.

"He had a played soccer when he was a kid in Germany," Prasse explained. "That was the whole book on why he didn't like our style of football."

"I Just Couldn't Believe It"

Erwin Prasse, who had been Nile Kinnick's teammate at Iowa, was serving in the military when he got the news.

"I just couldn't believe it when I heard that Nile had been killed," Prasse said. I thought it was a mistake because he was so perfect.

"He was the first pilot off the ship, and the first pilot was always the best one. But I guess there were problems with that airplane with oil pressure and that kind of stuff. Something malfunctioned.

"He made a perfect landing on the water and wasn't that far from his carrier. The boat was there in a moment."

But when the carrier, the USS *Lexington*, arrived at the scene, there was no sign of the plane or Kinnick.

George "Red" Frye, Kinnick's teammate and Iowa's center, was a pilot, too. He was an aviator in the Marine Corps who served in the South Pacific for 13 months.

"When Kinnick died, I was in cadet training at Corpus Christi, Texas," Frye said. "When I heard that Nile had died, I was in shock. As perfect as he was, I thought nothing would ever go wrong with him.

"But I guess, when the engine conks out, there's nothing you can do about it."

Last Time He Saw Kinnick

The last time Jim Hoak saw his friend, Nile Kinnick, was on August 2, 1941.

"That was the day my wife and I were married in Manchester, Iowa," Hoak said. "Nile was one of my ushers, and he was in his military uniform. I went into the military three months later."

Hoak said he was an ensign at a naval air station in Oregon when he learned of Kinnick's death.

"I had talked to him on the phone four weeks earlier," Hoak said. "He called to ask me a bunch of questions. He had some stuff—pictures and clippings—that I had my parents pack up and send to Nile's parents' place in Omaha."

Captain Skipped Spring Practice

Erwin Prasse, captain of the 1939 Ironmen, admits he and Coach Eddie Anderson "didn't hit it off right away."

After arriving in Iowa City, Anderson called Prasse in and began telling him what the team would be doing in spring practice.

"But I said, 'I'm sorry, Dr. Anderson, but I won't be out for spring practice,'" Prasse said. "He looked at me like I was kidding or that I was goofy. He then said, 'What? You're the captain of the team.'"

"I said, 'Yes, but I have an obligation to the baseball team. I bat cleanup most of the time.' Still, it didn't go over well with him that I didn't play in the spring. But I never thought spring football practice was worth anything except to hurt a bunch of people. I was happy to have an excuse not to show up."

George "Red" Frye, an Iowa center, participated in the 1939 spring practice and said, "I knew [Anderson] was going to be a perfectionist. One of the first things he said to us was that he didn't want any quitters.

"He said, 'If you're going to quit, quit now. Don't be bothering me for a certain amount of time, then back out.' I also recall him telling us, 'The team that's in the best condition is going to win the games.' He stressed conditioning."

Prasse said didn't have any problem with Anderson after shocking him by passing up spring practice in favor of baseball.

"He was a disciplinarian and we were eager," Prasse said. "The practice fields are usually higher in the middle, with kind of a mound there. We always ran plays uphill, and Nile Kinnick would run 10 yards further than the rest of us."

Ironmen Used No-Huddle Offense

The Ironmen usually employed a no-huddle offense, with quarterback Al Couppee calling the plays at the line of scrimmage.

"Couppee would call numbers like 43 and 82," end Erwin Prasse said. "We'd pick out the first digit of the first number and second digit of the second number, and that was the number of the play. Whatever came after that was a little diversion from it."

Coach Covered Big Ten Opener

When Iowa played Indiana on October 7 to start its Big Ten schedule in 1939, the man who covered the game for the *Waterloo* (Ia.) *Courier* was Leonard Raffensperger.

Raffensperger wasn't an employee of the newspaper, but he was an outstanding coach at East Waterloo High School. He later was Iowa's coach in 1950 and 1951.

"The *Waterloo Courier* sports editor in 1939 was a guy named Ed Moore, and he was a good friend of my dad," said Gene Raffensperger, Leonard's son and a man who is a former sports editor of the *Des Moines Register*. "He asked my dad if he'd cover the game.

"I don't know what caused Moore to do it, but he made a decision that he was going to go to Cedar Falls and cover the game Iowa State Teachers College [now Northern Iowa] played. Moore felt Iowa had been such a poor team the year before that nobody gave them a chance to do anything in 1939.

"I was only nine years old, but sat in the press box with my dad, who earlier in his life had toyed with the idea of being a journalist."

Leonard had a lot to write about on that hot afternoon. Iowa beat Indiana 32-29.

The 60-Minute Hawkeyes

Iowa's 1939 Ironmen got their name because so many of them played 60 minutes a game.

Nile Kinnick played a whopping 402 minutes out of a possible 480. And his impressive numbers that season didn't stop there. He was involved in scoring 107 of Iowa's 130 points that season.

"The fact that the team has been remembered for such a long time is not just because of Kinnick," standout end Erwin Prasse said. "That group of guys hung in those games for 60 minutes.

"When we beat Notre Dame, it was with 16 guys. Then Minnesota came to Iowa City the next week when Bernie Bierman had one of his great teams, and we beat those son-of-a-bucks with the same 16 guys. Minnesota pooped out."

Anderson Advertised for Help

Erwin Prasse, the standout captain and end on Iowa's 1939 team, said he was discussing with Coach Eddie Anderson one day what would take place at practice.

"This is no crap," Prasse said. "This guy, Wally Bergstrom, walked up to Anderson and told him he had answered an ad that Eddie had put in the *Daily Iowan*."

The *Daily Iowan* is the campus newspaper at Iowa.

"The ad talked about Anderson looking for people to come out for football and enjoy the sunshine and good weather of Iowa so they could help out the team," Prasse explained.

Anderson shook Bergstrom's right hand. But it was no ordinary handshake.

"Eddie had a habit of carrying some hard rubber balls in his coat pocket," Prasse explained. "He all the time was squeezing those things and developing a tremendous grip. He loved to put people on their knees when he shook their hands."

It turned out that Bergstrom had strong hands, too. And quite a grip.

"This guy had milked cows all of his life and had big hands," Prasse said. "Hell, I think his hands were as big as Michael Jordan's."

To Anderson, Bergstrom said: "I've never played football before. I grew up on a farm."

But he also had been off the farm for a while. Bergstrom had spent some time in 1938 working on a coffee boat in South America.

One thing led to another and Bergstrom, a 6'2", 205-pounder who had gone to high school in Olds, Iowa, south of Iowa City, became Anderson's second-team left tackle.

"When he was in the game, he played right next to me," Prasse said. "I had always kidded Jim Walker, the starting left tackle. I told him, 'You know, Jim, when you're playing next to me, they don't even need to send my suit out to be cleaned.'

"He cleared out all the interference and took care of everything," Prasse explained.

But then a problem arose.

"Walker hurt his leg against Michigan," Prasse explained, "and in comes Bergstrom to take his place. He had never played in front of anybody, and now we're in that big Michigan stadium and he has to line up next to me.

"I thought, 'My God, my mother is never going to recognize me after this.' Bergstrom had played a few minutes and was trying to find out what the hell to do when somebody hit him in the nose and broke it. Blood was streaming down his face. Then he got his Iowa dander up, and from that time on, he played 60 minutes a game.

"It was like having Jim Walker playing next to me. And, don't forget, Bergstom had never played football before—not even six-man football."

Despite Bergstrom's strong play off the bench, Iowa lost to Michigan 27-7.

But it was the only defeat those 1939 Ironmen suffered.

One other thing about that game on October 14 at Ann Arbor: In Michigan's backfield was a guy named Forest Evashevski, who later would coach the three best teams Iowa has ever had in modern-day football in 1956, 1958 and 1960.

"Typical All-American Boy"

Forest Evashevski, who was Michigan's blocker for Tom Harmon in the 1939 game against Iowa and later was the Hawkeyes' coach and athletic director, said Nile Kinnick "had a great day against us even though we had a convincing win."

Evashevski said Iowa "had a pretty good football team, but Harmon had a super game against them that day in 1939."

Of Kinnick, Evashevski said, "He didn't have great physical skills, but he was a complete player. He was awfully smart, didn't fumble and didn't hit the wrong hole. He was also a good defensive player.

"Another thing about Nile, he was a much better passer than his record indicates. I met him after we played against one another, and I don't say this because he's gone and is a past hero. If you had to name a typical all-American boy, it was Nile Kinnick."

Strangest Game

The strangest game Iowa played in 1939 was on November 4 at Purdue.

The Hawkeyes won 4-0 because right tackle Mike Enich, who was known as "Iron Mike," blocked two Purdue punts into the end zone for safeties.

Iowa really didn't need the second safety, people said afterward.

"We just wanted to make it decisive," line coach Jim Harris joked to the players.

End Erwin Prasse said Harris had another funny line after the game.

"Well, Enich hit a home run with the bases loaded," Harris told Prasse.

Significance of Notre Dame Game

Iowa's November 11, 1939 game against Notre Dame had special significance not only for the Hawkeyes as a team, but for halfback Nile Kinnick.

Indeed, Bill Reichardt—a former Iowa standout full-back who was a nine-year-old mascot (he says "nuisance") for the 1939 Hawkeyes—goes so far as to say Kinnick would not have won the Heisman Trophy had his team not beaten Notre Dame on a play fabricated in the huddle.

The game marked only the second time Iowa had played the Fighting Irish. The other game was on October 8, 1921, when Coach Howard Jones's Hawkeyes were early in a 20-game winning streak.

In the 1921 game, Coach Knute Rockne brought a Notre Dame team to Iowa City that hadn't lost since 1918. His captain and right end was Eddie Anderson, who would turn out to coach Kinnick and the rest of Iowa's players in 1939. The Hawkeyes won the 1921 game 10-7, scoring all of their points in the first quarter on Gordon Locke's touchdown and Aubrey Devine's field goal.

So, after an 18-year lapse, the Iowa-Notre Dame series was resumed in 1939. Elmer Layden, fullback on the famous "Four Horsemen" backfield at Notre Dame, was then the Irish coach. Anderson was in his first season at Iowa.

"I laugh about things that happened in that era," Erwin Prasse, Iowa's captain, recalls now. "Layden and Anderson, who were great friends, walked across the field before the game when we were loosening up.

"They met in the middle of the field and each of them was smoking a cigarette. Coaches and players had to sit on the bench in those days. You couldn't wander around the sidelines like those 150 guys on teams do today.

"Anderson smoked cigarettes during the game. You could always tell where he sat on the bench because there was a big mound of cigarette butts right under his legs. If two coaches walked onto the field today before a game and were smoking cigarettes, no one would believe it."

Iowa's only touchdown against Notre Dame came late in the first half when Nile Kinnick scored from the four-yard line.

Prasse, who was the Hawkeyes' starting left end, described the play to me this way:

"We had run some plays to the right, but couldn't score. We usually used a no-huddle offense, but when we couldn't score, quarterback Al Couppee called a huddle. He told Kinnick in the huddle, 'You're going to switch to right halfback and we're going to use the same play off-tackle to the left side.'

"We came out of the huddle, snapped the ball quickly, and Notre Dame didn't realize that Kinnick was the right halfback, and that's how he scored. Kinnick drop-kicked the extra point to put us ahead 7-0."

More than 60 years after the game was played, Reichardt gave me his version of the play. He said, "They originally called right halfback Buzz Dean's play in the huddle. But Dean said, 'I can't take it. I've got a separated shoulder.' Then they turned to Kinnick and said, 'Can you take it, Nile?'

Heisman Trophy finalist quarterback Brad Banks earned Big Ten and AP Player of the Year honors in 2002.
AP/WWP

HAWK SHOP®

THE UNIVERSITY OF IOWA

Locations

Iowa Hawk Shop
(Main Store)
Iowa Hawk Shop
1525 Highway 6 West
Coralville, Iowa

Iowa Hawk Shop
U of I Athletics Hall of Fame
2425 Prairie Meadow Dr.
Iowa City, Iowa

Health Science Store
Hospital Ramp 3,
Across from Kinnick Stadium
Iowa City, Iowa

University Book Store
Ground Floor,
Iowa Memorial Union
Iowa City, Iowa

Call
1-800-HAWK SHOP

Shop Online

www.HAWKSHOP.com

For custom Hawkeye merchandise click on...

CUST**⬤**M HAWK SHOP

Iowa football coach Kirk Ferentz was named Big Ten and AP Coach of the Year in 2002. *AP/WWP*

"Nile said, 'I think I've got a couple of broken ribs on my right side, so let's run the play to the left side.'"

Reichardt also claims Anderson was on the sideline shouting, 'Don't give the ball to Kinnick! Everybody in the stadium knows you're going to give it to him!'

"But against the rule of the coach—the meanest SOB around, I'm talking a mean, tough guy—they gave the ball to Kinnick," Reichardt said. "Those exhausted Iowa players leveled everybody on the field. Kinnick put the ball in his left hand, protected the ribs on his right side and crossed the goal line standing up.

"He then drop-kicked the extra point, and Iowa went on to win 7-6. Had that play failed and had Iowa not beaten Notre Dame, Kinnick would never have won the Heisman Trophy and they never would have named the stadium after him."

Reichardt says he obtained the information about the key play by hearing Anderson talk about the game several hours after its conclusion. Reichardt even claims Couppee had been replaced by another quarterback during that series of downs, but Prasse and teammate George "Red" Frye say that's not true.

In fact, Frye said Couppee played the entire game. Prasse said he also played the entire game.

"Before he died, Couppee told me he wasn't in the game on that play," Reichardt said.

"Our family lived two blocks from Anderson's home. I was a good friend of Nick Anderson, Eddie's son, and spent a lot of time in their home. At 8 o'clock on Saturday night, after the Iowa-Notre Dame game had finished, I heard Eddie talking about how he told the guy calling signals to not give the ball to Kinnick."

But he did it anyway.

In the game, Prasse said the Ironmen used 16 players. Eight of them went all 60 minutes.

NILE KINNICK SCORES AGAINST NOTRE DAME

Anderson Turned into a Prophet

George "Red" Frye, a center on Iowa's 1939 team, recalls a meeting Coach Eddie Anderson had with his Iowa players a few nights before the key game against Notre Dame.

"Eddie would have a chalk talk every night," Frye explained. "We'd practice at a field over by the stadium, then walk across the campus to the Memorial Union, where we had our training table. Then we'd walk up the hill to Macbride Hall, where the coach would kind of prep us."

Frye said an interesting exchange between Anderson and Bill Gallagher, a reserve quarterback, took place at the chalk talk on Wednesday night of the week the Hawkeyes were to play Notre Dame.

Frye called Gallagher "kind of the comic of the outfit."

Suddenly, Anderson turned to Gallagher and said, "Willie, how bad are we going to beat Notre Dame? How bad do we want to beat 'em?"

"Forty to nothing," Gallagher quickly said.

"Hell, no," Anderson responded. "It's going to be 7-6 and they'll remember it the rest of their lives."

How Many Teams Did Iowa Play?

Included among the spectators at the 1939 Iowa-Notre Dame game were Leonard Raffensperger and his wife, Leone.

Raffensperger was a successful high school coach in Waterloo, Iowa, and later was Iowa's coach in 1950 and 1951.

"My dad told me that when the Iowa-Notre Dame game started, Iowa was wearing its usual black jerseys with gold numbers," said Gene Raffensperger, Leonard's son. "Notre Dame came out wearing navy blue jerseys.

"The officials let the game start. I don't know if Iowa protested or if the referees said, 'This is just not right. Those teams look too much alike.'

"When Notre Dame's players came out for the last half, they were wearing green jerseys. My dad said there was a guy sitting near him who had had a few drinks in the first half. So here comes Notre Dame out of the tunnel wearing green and this guy said, 'Well, @#$%, who are we playing now?' as though there was another team on the field."

Couppee Was "Outstanding"

Erwin Prasse, the left end and captain of Iowa's 1939 team, said Al Couppee was an outstanding quarterback.

"I'd rate him a greater quarterback than Forest Evashevski of Michigan," Prasse said. "And I say that even though Michigan gave us our only loss in 1939."

Evashevski became Iowa's coach in 1952, and his 1956, 1958 and 1960 Hawkeye teams were the best the university has ever had.

The Young Bob Brooks

In 1939, Bob Brooks was a 13-year-old student at Franklin Junior High School in Cedar Rapids, Iowa.

His father, Ira, was an Iowa sports fan who became a season football ticket holder in 1939. Young Bob loved tagging along with his parents to Iowa City for Hawkeye games.

This is the same Bob Brooks who would later make his mark in the University of Iowa athletic scene. He became a play-by-play radio broadcaster, did Hawkeye football games for 55 years for Iowa stations and, in 2002, was presented with the Chris Schenkel Award as a member of the College Football Hall of Fame.

"I saw my first Iowa game in 1938," Brooks said. "Iowa played Colgate and lost 14-0."

But then came 1939. It was Coach Eddie Anderson's first season and Nile Kinnick's last season.

Asked when he could see the magic developing that year, Brooks said, "Well, Iowa beat South Dakota 41-0 in the opener, and nobody knew who Nile Kinnick was, to speak of. Then the game that kind of got things rolling was the next one against Indiana, which Iowa won 32-29.

Erwin Prasse, who caught the winning touchdown pass from Kinnick against the Hoosiers, said it was so hot "that it seemed like 100 degrees in the shade. I lost 18 pounds that day, and Kinnick lost 12."

Iowa football was still not a big hit. Only 20,000 fans were in the stadium, but the Hawkeyes were fashioning a personality. They passed up what would have been a likely tying field goal to go for the critical touchdown against Indiana. People liked that.

"I had one foot in the end zone and one foot out of the end zone," Prasse said of the winning play. "But the pass counted."

Brooks said he saw most of Iowa's home games in 1939 as a member of the Knothole Club.

"Kids got in for 25 cents for the season, and that enabled us to stand or sit in the end zone," said Brooks, who added that those in the Knothole Club would jump the fence and go into the grandstand.

Brooks talked of the two big national headline-makers on Iowa's schedule—the successive home games against Notre Dame and Minnesota.

"What I remember about the Notre Dame game is that I thought I probably wasn't going to see it," he commented.

"All of a sudden, it was evident the Iowa athletic department was going to sell out the game.

"So the kids' Knothole Club was canceled. My parents had two tickets to the game, but I didn't have one. I believe tickets then cost $5, and I remember sitting around the evening dinner table at home when the subject came up as to how I was going to get a ticket to the game. I didn't have $5.

"So I finally contracted with a neighbor to mow his lawn for the next year to earn my five bucks."

Brooks said the Knothole Club was restored for the November 18 game against Minnesota, a team that had beaten Iowa eight consecutive times. But the stadium was so jammed that it could have been sold out without selling discount tickets to kids.

"I stood under a sumac tree in the north end zone," Brooks recalled.

"Bill Green caught the winning touchdown pass from Kinnick, and Iowa won 13-9.

"Minnesota was a national power, and Bernie Bierman, its coach, was the Bear Bryant of his time. After the game, the field was flooded with fans, and I was down there, too.

"I watched Bierman come off the field. I thought, by the look on his face, that the bricks in the stadium were going to crack. He was boiling mad."

Kinnick Introduced Willkie

George Mills of Des Moines, a longtime wire service, newspaper, magazine and television reporter, got firsthand knowledge of Nile Kinnick's public speaking ability in 1940.

"I was in Iowa Falls when Wendell Willkie was the Republican nominee for president," Mills told me as his 97th birthday approached. "His special train stopped there for a big rally in the city park.

"Kinnick, who I believe was then a law student at Iowa, was there. He introduced Willkie and made a very nice speech. In fact, it was a beautiful speech.

"I remember saying then that the guy could well go the route of his grandfather—George W. Clarke—and become the governor of Iowa."

Chapter 3
The Forest Evashevski Years

Evashevski Becomes Iowa's Coach

He played against Iowa when he was a blocker for Tom Harmon at Michigan.

In his early 30s, he was already making his mark as a strong collegiate coach at Washington State.

Iowa noticed.

Iowa hired him to rebuild its sagging football fortunes following the 1951 season.

Forest Evashevski was his name.

Paul Brechler, who then was Iowa's athletic director, called Evashevski after the Hawkeyes finished a 2-5-2 season in 1951. But there was competition for him, so Brechler had to act quickly

And he got his man. Some earlier time he had spent in Iowa City during World War II made Evashevski's decision easier.

"I spent a year at Iowa in pre-flight school and played for the Iowa Seahawks," he explained. "So I knew quite a bit about the university and the athletic program. Then there was the factor was that I wanted to coach in the Big Ten. That was home to me.

"That plus the fact they'd had such a bad record at Iowa, you knew people were going to be patient with me."

Evashevski wound up building a 52-27-4 record as Iowa's coach from 1952-1960. His 1956 and 1958 teams won outright Big Ten championships and were victorious in the Rose Bowl. His 1960 team tied Minnesota for the conference title.

Ranked in order of strength, the 1958 team that had an 8-1-1 record and led the nation in total offense, the 1956 team that went 9-1 and the 1960 team that went 8-1 are regarded as the best in modern football history at Iowa.

Randy Duncan, who played for Evashevski and was a consensus all-America quarterback, said, "I'm not sure we didn't have a better team in 1957 than we had in 1958."

However, the 1957 squad, which finished No. 5 in the final United Press International rankings and No. 6 in the Associated Press rankings, lost to Ohio State, was tied by Michigan, and didn't play in the Rose Bowl.

Evashevski retired as the Hawkeyes' coach at the young age of 43 and became the school's athletic director.

Long after Evashevski coached his final game and long after his days as Iowa's athletic director, veteran sportscaster Bob Brooks of Cedar Rapids recalled what made him successful.

"I think Evashevski had a command presence about him," Brooks said. "When he walked into a room, people noticed him. He was an innovator. He had a lot of genius about him regarding college football.

"He was one of very few coaches who could change the game plan at halftime and make it work. He was a great motivator."

Jim Zabel, who broadcast Iowa games on the radio for 50 years at WHO in Des Moines, said Evashevski was "a genius as an Xs and Os man. He was a great organizer with tremendous vision and imagination.

"He could change the whole offense in a week. He had a touch of magic. And he knew how to deal with players, with management, and the big-money guys."

Imaginative and Creative

Chalmers "Bump" Elliott, who was on Evashevski's original coaching staff at Iowa in 1952 and later was the university's athletic director from 1970-1991, said "imagination and the ability to adjust" were among Evashevski's strengths.

"He was very creative," Elliott said. "He had a great sense of timing. He knew when to make a move and when to do things. If, in practice, the team was tired—and he sensed that very nicely and readily—he would tell the players, 'Oh, go on in and have a Coke.'

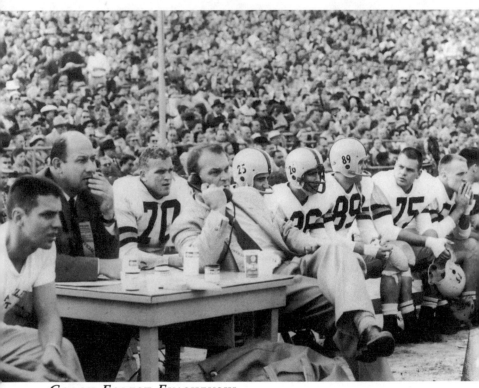

Coach Forest Evashevski

"He did unusual things and really did a good job with the material he had."

Elliott was listed as Iowa's backfield coach, but said he also was in charge of the Hawkeyes' linebackers under Evashevski.

"Evy [the nickname nearly everyone used for Evashevski] had only four varsity assistants," Elliott said. "The others were Whitey Piro, Bob Flora and Archie Kodros."

Woody Hayes Threw His Coat

Forest Evashevski's first season as Iowa's coach got off to a lackluster start.

The 1952 Hawkeyes lost their first four games to Pittsburgh, Indiana, Purdue and Wisconsin by the combined score of 129-54.

Powerful Ohio State, coached by Woody Hayes, was next on the schedule. The game was played October 25 in Iowa City.

It was a date that was very important in Evashevski's coaching tenure and in the history of football at the university.

In a shocking upset that would set the tone for Evashevski's future seasons at Iowa, the Hawkeyes unbelievably won the game 8-0.

A half-century after the game was played, I asked Evashevski if he had any idea his team would pull off the monster victory.

"No," he said. "In fact, I was afraid we might get really clobbered because we gambled so much. I think if Woody had started throwing the ball early, Ohio State could have gotten us out of the defense we were in.

"We jammed up to stop their running game, and I knew Woody was stubborn enough to keep trying—and he did. Fortunately, they didn't start throwing the ball until it was too late."

Bump Elliott, who was in his first season as Iowa's backfield coach, recalls the Ohio State game as being very unusual.

"I would say it was on Tuesday in the week of the game that Evy came up with the idea, and we developed as a staff, to change the whole offense from the Michigan single-wing and T-formation that we were using," Elliott explained.

"Before the Ohio State game, we went to an unbalanced line, split-T formation, with big splits in the line. The linemen were two yards from each other, and it looked like we were spread clear across the field.

"We came in with a very limited passing game off of it—some hook passes, some swing passes to the halfbacks. It was nothing exceptional, but the fact we changed the whole thing made it work. The other thing that was significant was that the offense learned to call the plays at the line of scrimmage, depending on where the defense lined up."

Elliott said, "We'd come to the line of scrimmage, look it over, then call a play that would go to the open hole of the defense. I think everything upset Ohio State so much that they forgot about their own offense and we stopped them.

"If Ohio State had tended to their business, they probably could have moved the ball better. But they got frustrated with their running game and passing game. We also changed the defense for Ohio State. We went into a five-man front after using a variety of six- and five-man fronts earlier."

Elliott said it was during the game that the frustrated Hayes took off his sportcoat and threw it into the grandstand that is not far from the visitors' bench in Iowa's stadium.

"The fans weren't going to give it back, but they finally did," Elliott said.

Opening the Recruiting Doors

Forest Evashevski, Iowa's highly successful coach from 1952-1960, said the 8-0 victory over Ohio State in his first season stands out as "the one that got us on our way. That opened up the recruiting opportunity.

"People heard of us. We got a look at some of the better high school players. I think the second Rose Bowl game, when we beat California, stood out, too."

Iowa's 1958 team, which routed California 38-12, led the nation in total offense, was ranked No. 1 nationally by the Football Writers Association of America and was No. 2 behind Louisiana State in the final Associated Press poll."

Bump Elliott and the Rose Bowl

Bump Elliott, who was an Iowa assistant football coach from 1952-1956 and returned to be the university's athletic director from 1970-1991, has quite a distinction.

He's the only person to go to the Rose Bowl in five capacities. He went as a Michigan player, an Iowa assistant coach, Michigan's head coach, Michigan's assistant athletic director and Iowa's athletic director.

BUMP ELLIOTT

The Car Stopped, Cal Jones Got In

It's a good thing that car stopped at Cal Jones's home at Steubenville, Ohio, in 1952.

In the car were Frank Gilliam and Eddie Vincent, who went on to outstanding careers under Forest Evashevski at Iowa.

Gilliam, an end, and Vincent, a running back, were part of Evashevski's first recruiting class. They were two-thirds of what was to be known as the "Steubenville Trio."

The story goes that Gilliam and Vincent had their car packed with luggage when they happened to stop by the home of Jones on their way out of Steubenville.

The thinking was that Jones, an outstanding guard, was headed to Ohio State, where he'd play for Woody Hayes.

While Gilliam and Vincent were preparing to say goodbye to Jones, the big lineman said, "Hey, wait a minute. I'm going with you."

Suddenly, Jones put some of his belongings together and jumped into the car with Gilliam and Vincent.

Seeing that, Jones's mother said from the front porch, "Calvin, you can't go to Iowa City. Mr. Hayes is counting on you to be on team at Ohio State."

Gilliam confirmed the story in a conversation with me while attending an Iowa game in 2002.

"Mrs. Jones was a woman of her word," Gilliam said.

However, that didn't stop Jones. Into the car he went, and off it drove to Iowa City.

"I know I promised Coach Hayes that I would go to Ohio State," Jones told his mother, "but I want to go to Iowa."

Jones later became the first two-time consensus All-American in Iowa history and won the 1955 Outland Trophy that was awarded to the nation's top interior lineman. In all, he was named to 22 All-America teams, and he was a first-team All-Big Ten player in all three of his varsity seasons. In 1955, Jones was Iowa's captain.

Jones died as the result of a plane crash in Canada on December 9, 1956.

His uniform, No. 62, is one of two retired by the university. The only other player whose number has been retired was Heisman Trophy winner Nile Kinnick, who wore No. 24.

Jones was inducted into the inaugural class of Iowa's Lettermen's Hall of Fame, and he also was a standout in the classroom. Jones, a physical education major, had a 3.0 grade-point average.

Evashevski, who called Jones "the greatest lineman I ever coached," told me there is truth to the story about how the big guy wound up at Iowa.

"Ohio State had Cal sewed up, and they weren't interested in Gilliam or Vincent," Evashevski said. "It was on the recommendation of a high school coach that we took Gilliam and Vincent.

"When they decided to come to Iowa, Jones was a little reluctant to go alone to Ohio State. If he came to Iowa, he'd have his two friends with him. We told him he could room with the other two players, and that did it— he hopped into the car and came with them."

Cal Jones

California, Here We Come

Frank Gilliam, who lettered as an end in 1953, 1954 and 1956, said the game he had the fondest memories of was Iowa's 6-0 victory over Ohio State in 1956.

That one gave Coach Forest Evashevski's Hawkeyes the Big Ten championship and sent them to their first Rose Bowl.

The only points came on Kenny Ploen's 17-yard touchdown pass to Jim Gibbons in the third quarter. Bob Prescott, however, missed his first extra point of the season.

"Gibbons was a real good football player," Evashevski says now. "He didn't have great speed, but in those days you went both ways and Jim was a good defensive player as well as offensive player. He was mainly a good blocker, but he did have good hands."

Ohio State never got inside Iowa's 32-yard line. The Buckeyes managed only 147 yards rushing and 18 yards passing against Iowa's relentless defense.

"I felt very good about beating them because they were a good team and we were a good team," Gilliam said. "There was a lot of good hitting. The score didn't indicate the caliber of the football game."

Although he was from Steubenville, Ohio, Gilliam said he got no particular thrill in beating Ohio State.

"Once I left the state of Ohio, that was it," he explained. "I didn't have any friends on the Ohio State team. I had some friends on the Indiana team, but Ohio State was just another game for me."

Gilliam said Hayes "tried to get me to go to Ohio State, but my recruiting trip to Iowa City was a very positive experience, and I remember telling Eddie Vincent—my teammate and friend from Steubenville—that "I don't know what you're going to do, but I'm pretty certain this is where I'm going to school."

KENNY PLOEN

Milo Hamilton's Memories

Milo Hamilton, a Hall of Fame baseball announcer, called some interesting games while broadcasting Iowa football games on KSTT in Davenport in the 1950s.

"My biggest memory was Iowa's 8-0 win over Ohio State in 1952," he said. "Coach Forest Evashevski changed his offense early in the week to the wing-T, and then it became his bread and butter.

"Ohio State didn't have a clue. In fact, I think that game was the beginning of the 'I hate you, Evy' stuff by Woody. That win gave the whole state of Iowa something to cheer about after Evy inherited a pretty rag-tag team."

Hamilton said his most disappointing football game was the tie with Notre Dame in 1953 "when Notre Dame called all of those phony timeouts."

Alex Karras "Hated Evashevski"

One of the more interesting guys to play football for Iowa in the Forest Evashevski coaching era was Alex Karras, who lettered in 1956 and 1957.

He was a consensus All-American, won the 1957 Outland Trophy given to the nation's top interior lineman, and then went on to an outstanding NFL career after being chosen by the Detroit Lions in the first round of the 1958 draft.

However, despite the big tackle's outstanding ability and the success of his Iowa teams, he didn't get along with Evashevski and he didn't enjoy his years in Iowa City.

"Karras hated Evashevski, and he still does," quarterback Randy Duncan, a teammate of Karras, recalls now. "I think Karras hated Evy for a lot of reasons. Evy was on everybody's back, and he was on Karras's back big-time.

"Karras was a great football player, but he didn't really like offense and, in those days, you had to go both ways. So he didn't block anybody. What he wanted to do was chase down quarterbacks and play defense. Alex has no good memories of Iowa."

Bill Reichardt, the former standout fullback at Iowa who starred just before Evashevski became Iowa's coach, said he, too, is familiar with Karras's problems at Iowa.

"Evashevski was a bully," Reichardt said. "Karras had a mind of his own. He didn't do everything Evashevski wanted him to do, and Evashevski was on him all the time. So Alex totally disliked him."

How Karras wound up at Iowa is a story in itself. Karras has told teammates and other friends that Evashevski came to his brother's home in Gary, Indiana, and had him flown to Spencer, Iowa, where he stayed for one month. Why Spencer, a small city in northwest Iowa? Because, Karras thought, recruiters from other schools wouldn't know where Spencer was.

"Alex told me once that, because of what happened to him, he was going to write a book, call it Kidnapped, and put it on the screen," Duncan said of a guy who became an actor after his days in the NFL.

I asked Evashevski what he thought of Karras, and he praised him.

"Karras was a great football player—mainly defensively," Evashevski said. "We had better tackles over the years offensively than Karras, but I don't think anyone was any better defensively than Alex."

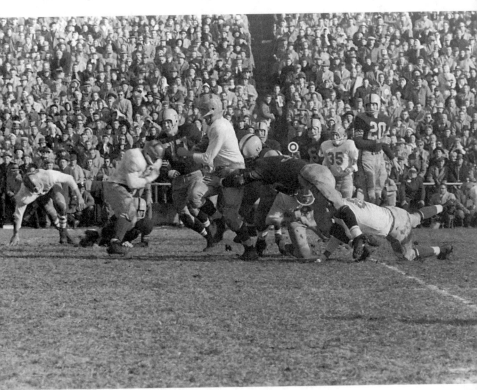

ALEX KARRAS

Duncan Almost Quit

The 1958 team was the best in the last half-century of Iowa football, and the quarterback who passed brilliantly that season was Randy Duncan.

The Hawkeyes finished with an 8-1-1 record, won the Big Ten championship, walloped California 38-12 in the Rose Bowl, finished No. 2 in the final Associated Press and United Press International polls, and led the nation in total offense.

Duncan was a consensus all-American and the most valuable player at Iowa and in the Big Ten. He finished second in the Heisman Trophy voting, led the Big Ten in passing and is a member of the National Football Foundation Hall of Fame.

"Randy was a great passer," said Forest Evashevski, who was his coach. "He didn't have the speed of Kenny Ploen [who had quarterbacked Iowa's 1956 Rose Bowl champions] and wasn't the defensive back Kenny was. But Randy was the better passer."

However, Duncan now says he almost quit the team in his sophomore season.

"Bump Elliott, the backfield coach, recruited me," Duncan said. "He was a good guy. He was the only reason I went to Iowa.

"Evashevski was a mean SOB. He constantly berated me and was on my back. I was thinking about quitting. I went to Bump and said, 'Bump, I don't know if I can take this any more. This guy is on my back all the time. He never lets up.'

RANDY DUNCAN

"Bump said, 'I'll tell you something, Randy. When he gets off your back is when you should start worrying.'"

Duncan said Iowa had an outstanding team in 1958 for a number of reasons.

"First of all, we were running the wing-T offense, and defenses hadn't learned to cope with it," he explained. "And we had a lot of speed. Evashevski put the offense in for the 1956 season, but the '56 team had a running offense with no wideouts and slotbacks.

"Look at the halfbacks we had in 1958—Ray Jauch, Kevin Furlong, Bobby Jeter and Willie Fleming."

Duncan said a 13-13 tie with Air Force in the second game was the key to the season.

"We thought we were going to kill those guys," he said. "They were a bunch of little guys—most of them juniors. But it turned out that the game made our season. After that, we really started playing hard. But we did get beat by Ohio State. On that day, they were a better team."

Of the Rose Bowl romp over California, Duncan said, "It wasn't even a game."

Jeter ran for 194 yards on only nine carries, and Fleming had 85 yards in nine carries as the Hawkeyes set Rose Bowl records for total offense (516 yards) and rushing offense (429). Jeter scored on an 81-yard touchdown dash.

Fleming's Short Career

Willie Fleming wasn't at Iowa very long, but what an impression he made.

"Willie was the best running back I had at Iowa," Coach Forest Evashevski said of the player who played only in the 1958 season before encountering academic problems.

"It's too bad he didn't finish his career at Iowa, because I think he would have had all of the records in his pocket if he would have. He was a great football player."

Fleming scored touchdowns on runs of 37 and seven yards in the Hawkeyes' 38-12 Rose Bowl victory over California.

"Fainting Irish" Tie Iowa

One of the most bizarre games in Forest Evashevski's nine seasons as Iowa's coach was in the 1953 finale against Notre Dame at South Bend, Indiana.

The game ended in a 14-14 tie, but only after Notre Dame had resorted to tactics that had people calling its players the "Fainting Irish."

Just before each half ended, assorted Notre Dame players collapsed on the field so the officials would stop the clock. Consequently, the Irish scored touchdowns in the final seconds of each half.

Iowa coaches, players and fans thought the phony injuries robbed them of an opportunity to score a huge upset. When he returned to Iowa City, Evashevski pounced on the "Fainting Irish" theme by paraphrasing the words of sportswriter Grantland Rice with these words:

"When the One Great Scorer comes
to write against our name,
He won't ask that we won or lost,
But how we got gypped at Notre Dame."

"The 'Fainting Irish' game is one that will stick in my mind forever," said Jim Zabel of Des Moines, who was an Iowa play-by-play radio announcer for a half-century and was in the press box for the game.

"Vee Green, a former coach at Drake University, was my color commentator in those years, and he picked up on what was going on right away during the broadcast. When he saw Notre Dame's players falling on the ground, Vee said, 'There's something about this that I don't like. That man is not injured.'"

Bob Brooks, the longtime Iowa broadcaster from Cedar Rapids, also did the play-by-play of that game and said the fainting by the Irish players to stop the clock "in retrospect, was common in those days. That's what teams did—anything to get a timeout.

"However, it was a little abnormal that Frank Leahy, who then was Notre Dame's coach, had the Irish fainting all over the place. Players went down like they were shot. However, as I remember my broadcast of the game, I didn't make a major issue out of the fainting because it seemed to happen a lot in football in those days.

"But after the game, the New York press picked up on it. Grantland Rice and other national media people took Notre Dame and Leahy to task for playing for a tie, and maybe doing it illegally."

The national attention certainly didn't hurt Evashevski and his players, who finished with a 5-3-1 record. Iowa wound up ninth in the final Associated Press rankings—the first time a Hawkeye football team had been rated since 1939.

"I Figured He Must Be a Genius"

Al Grady, who was a longtime sports editor of the *Iowa City Press-Citizen*, said he attended Iowa's practices nearly every day during Forest Evashevski's nine seasons as coach.

"During those practices, Evy would almost always come up and visit with me and other reporters," Grady said. "I figured he must be a genius because he'd be talking to me and laughing—saying something like, 'Do you know what happened at our house last night?'

"I'd say, 'No.'

"Evy continued with, 'Ruth was doing this' and then all of a sudden, he would scream, 'Jim Gibbons, get your head in the game, you jackass! Run the play again and make yourself available for the pass.'

"Then Evy would continue talking about his wife, Ruth. He'd say, 'She spilled the spaghetti on the floor.'"

Grady explained that Evashevski "wasn't even watching and he saw out of the corner of his eye that Gibbons didn't run a precise route."

Grady also recalled another incident at one of Evashevski's practices. It involved John Nocera, a fullback who was Iowa's captain in 1958.

"Evy called out something, and Nocera called the team together," Grady said. "Nocera said, "'OK, we ain't gonna do that any more.'

"Evy then blew his whistle and said, 'John, it's "we're not going to do that any more.""

Evashesvki then turned to Grady and said, "You not only have to teach football, you've got to teach English."

Field Turned into a Quagmire

Forest Evashevski's 1957 Iowa team opened its Big Ten season at Indiana.

"It hadn't rained there in three weeks," quarterback Randy Duncan recalls now. "But the field was all muddy—an absolute quagmire. Evashevski went nuts. He said, 'I've never had a coach [Bob Hicks was the Hoosiers' coach in 1957] do this to me in all my years of football. The guy watered down the field. This is the worst thing I've ever had done to me.'

"By that time, Evashevski had smoke coming out of his ears. So we go out and kill Indiana 47-7, and we're on the plane coming home."

Duncan said he sat next to Bob Flora, one of Evashevski's assistant coaches, on the plane.

"Flora said, 'God, this game reminded me of when we were playing Notre Dame in 1954.'

"I asked him why it reminded him of that. He said, 'Well, hell, Evashevski called up all the coaches at midnight the night before the game and we went out and watered the field all night long.'"

So watering the field wasn't new after all. By the way, Notre Dame won that game in Iowa City, 34-18.

One-Handed Catch

Those who watched quarterback Randy Duncan direct Iowa's potent offense in 1958 recall the one-handed catch Curt Merz made in a 26-20 homecoming victory over Northwestern.

"It was a drop-back pass," Duncan explained. "I was chased out of the pocket, and Merz went up and got the ball with one hand in the end zone."

One Job or the Other

Forest Evashevski retired as Iowa's football coach at the relatively young age of 43.

He had records of 9-1, 7-1-1, 8-1-1, 5-4 and 8-1 in the final five years of his nine-year stay as coach. Included were two Rose Bowl victories.

He had wanted to serve as both Iowa's coach and athletic director, but the university's Board in Control of Athletics wouldn't allow it. Evashevski had to choose one job or the other.

"In those days, people at the Big Ten schools thought the athletic director and the football coach had to be two different people," said George Wine, who was hired by Evashevski to be Iowa's sports information director in 1968 and stayed in the job until 1993, long after Evashevski left.

"The Iowa Board told him, 'Take your pick,' and he took the athletic director job."

Brechler had resigned to become the first commissioner of the Western Athletic Conference.

"Evashevski went to war with Brechler and got his job," explained Wine, "But I really think the athletic director job bored him because it was too easy for him. I think he wanted to get the football coaching job back— there wasn't much doubt about that, but he never got it back because he wouldn't give up the athletic director job.

"I call that the dumbest decision the Athletic Board has ever made. If they had let him go ahead and coach the football team and be the athletic director, there's no telling what he'd have done. He was in his prime and was dominating the Big Ten."

Wine said Evashevski "could have put together a tremendous program as Iowa's athletic director had he not let some of the personal skirmishes he had interfere with that—namely, of course, the one with football coach Ray Nagel.

"Evashevski was exceptionally dynamic—maybe the most dynamic guy I've ever been around. When he came into a room, things stopped. And he had the ability to make rapid-fire decisions. That always impressed me."

Jerry Burns, who immediately succeeded Evashevski as coach, lasted only five seasons. It was his 4-5 record in

1962 that started a string of 19 consecutive non-winning seasons for the Hawkeyes.

A long-lasting feud between Evashevski and Nagel, who was Iowa's coach from 1966-1970, resulted in both men leaving their jobs at Iowa. Evashevski resigned as athletic director in the spring of 1970 and Nagel's contract as coach was not renewed after a 3-6-1 record the following fall.

Indeed, those were dark days in the football program at Iowa.

And things didn't get better until a Texan named Hayden Fry came to the rescue.

Chapter 4
The Hayden Fry Years

"My Favorite Place is Iowa"

Hayden Fry, who became Iowa's winningest football coach with a record of 143-89-6 from 1979-1998, received what he called "without question the biggest honor I've ever been fortunate to attain" when he was named to the College Football Hall of Fame in March 2003.

Fry joined a list of 15 former Iowa coaches, players and administrators in the Hall of Fame.

"I've been very lucky at many junctures of my life, and this is a prime example of how blessed I've been," Fry said. "I've been associated with many good people at Southern Methodist, North Texas State and the University of Iowa. But, without question, my favorite place was and still is Iowa.

"The assistants, fans and everybody associated with Iowa football are the main reason this is happening to me. I owe much to everyone I've worked for and with during my career. But what happened at Iowa is the primary reason I've been given this honor. Part of this award belongs to the people of Iowa and, for that, I will be eternally grateful."

Kirk Ferentz, Iowa's present coach, said he called Fry to congratulate him about being named to the Hall of Fame.

"That's one of the highest honors anyone can get who does what we do," Ferentz said. "He was thrilled to death. He said he flipped his golf cart when he found out about it."

Other Iowa coaches previously named to the Hall of Fame were Howard Jones, Dr. Eddie Anderson, Edward "Slip" Madigan and Forest Evashevski.

The former Iowa players in the Hall are Nile Kinnick, who won the 1939 Heisman Trophy, Gordon Locke, Fred "Duke" Slater, Calvin Jones, Earl Banks, Aubrey Devine, Randy Duncan, Alex Karras and Chuck Long.

The former Iowa administrator in the Hall is Eric Wilson, who was the university's first sports information director.

1981 Hawkeyes Go to Pasadena

On November 21, 1981, something happened in Kinnick Stadium that jolted the collegiate football world and touched off pandemonium in an entire state.

Iowa, which hadn't produced a winning football record since 1961 and had been showing plenty of signs of never being able to solve the "Big Two, Little Eight" dominance of the Big Ten that Ohio State and Michigan had created, pulled off what football have-nots always dream of doing.

Hayden Fry's Hawkeyes got a huge assist from Ohio State and won a ticket to the 1982 Rose Bowl. Iowa did its part by mauling Michigan State 36-7. Ohio State opened the door for Fry and his players earlier in the day by winning at Michigan 14-9.

Although Iowa and Ohio State finished the regular season with 8-3 records and tied for first place in the conference at 6-2, the Hawkeyes got the bid to Pasadena because the Buckeyes had been to the Rose Bowl more recently.

I still vividly recall the bedlam in the stadium that afternoon. It was a day when the Hawkeyes defied all the odds and performed with a heart and soul unseen in Iowa City since the 1950s.

Phil Blatcher, a senior who began the season as Iowa's third-string tailback, ran for 247 yards as his team earned the right to play Washington on January 1 in the Rose Bowl.

I had been hospitalized in Iowa City earlier in November and was starting to regain my strength when I covered the Iowa-Michigan State game.

"I think this game brought me back to life," I told another sportswriter in the press box.

Know what? It brought an entire football program back to life, too.

Coaches' Graveyard

Until Hayden Fry arrived, Iowa had one of the sorriest collegiate football programs in the nation from 1961-1978.

If anything resembled a "coaches' graveyard," this was it.

I covered a number of Hawkeye games during those years. It was not a fun time.

Iowa went through four coaches in that period. Jerry Burns, who succeeded Forest Evashevski in 1961, had only one winning season—he was 5-4 in his break-in year. He was fired after beating only Oregon State in a 10-game season in 1965.

I recall sitting outside closed-door meetings when Burns's fate was being decided. For him, the news was not good.

Ray Nagel lasted five years. He was at Iowa during a tumultuous time. Nagel seemed ready to turn the corner in 1968, but a boycott of spring practice by a number of black players had an influence that carried into the 1969 season and afterward.

Trying to learn of Nagel's job status, I had several shouting matches with him before he was finally shown the door by his bosses.

Adding to the problems at that time, there was a tremendous amount of turmoil between Nagel and Evashevski, who then was Iowa's athletic director. Evashevski resigned in the spring of 1970, and Nagel's contract as coach was not renewed after a 3-6-1 record in the fall of that year.

Frank Lauterbur lasted only three years as coach, going 1-10 in 1971, 3-7-1 in 1972 and an embarrassing 0-11 in 1973.

On the day he was fired, Lauterbur held an umbrella over my head so he could protect the notepad I was using from the rain that was falling near the stadium. He was a good guy, but Iowa clearly was not the right place for him.

That wasn't the last bleak day. Bob Commings, who had played for Evashevski at Iowa in 1953, 1956 and 1957, was fired after five seasons as coach in 1978.

After the season finale, a 42-7 loss at Michigan State on November 25, I followed him as he made the slow walk off a Big Ten field for the last time. He had already been told his fate. He was history at Iowa.

Hayden Fry Makes a Decision

After 17 consecutive seasons of non-winning football under four coaches, Iowa athletic director Bump Elliott and other university officials were ready to talk to another leader, and Hayden Fry was willing to listen.

Fry had already spent 11 seasons as the coach at Southern Methodist and six at North Texas State. His last two years at North Texas State produced records of 10-1 and 9-2, but hardly anyone noticed in a state that was dominated by larger universities.

"We had those outstanding records and beat a lot of great teams, but didn't get invited to any bowl games," Fry told me. "In addition, I had been the football coach and athletic director at both SMU and North Texas State, and I decided I didn't want any more administrative work.

"I wanted to go to a school that was the University of..."

In other words, he wanted to coach at a high-profile state university that might be able to have some football impact.

"I told my staff that we were going someplace, and we began looking at film," Fry said. "We wound up considering Oklahoma State, Ole Miss and Iowa. One day I went to the coaches' room and the assistants were watching film of Iowa."

Fry was surprised when Bill Brashier, a member of his staff, spoke up.

"Coach Fry," Brashier said, "we've made up our mind. We took a vote and we want to go to Iowa."

"Iowa?" Fry said. "We don't even know where Iowa is located."

"Sit down here and look at this film," Brashier told Fry. "The game on the film was played at Kinnick Stadium in Iowa City, Iowa made a first down and all the fans in the stands jumped up and applauded. It was unbelievable."

Fry said the assistants were in agreement when one of them asked, "What would have happened if they made a touchdown?"

Anyway, Fry said the crowd reaction was one thing that motivated the North Texas State staff to come to Iowa.

"For me, the big factor was Bump Elliott, who was Iowa's athletic director and a great person. And, to this day, I've never read the contract. I didn't even know how much they were paying me or how long it was for.

"I just shook Bump's hand."

COACH HAYDEN FRY

Time for Some Excitement

Hayden Fry was hired as Iowa's coach in December 1978, and athletic director Bump Elliott figured he had the right guy.

"Hayden had a great instinct for being a head coach," Elliott said. "He was a strong leader. He always thought highly of the Marine Corps, and I think he felt himself a captain in the marines and his team was his unit.

"He did a great job. He had a great sense of humor, but he could be tough when he wanted to be. Hayden was very sound, very good with players, and they really responded to him. He also was a coaches' coach."

Fry took over the Iowa program after a period of little razzle-dazzle on offense. So anything different that he did would look good to Iowa's loyal fans.

"Iowa had been criticized heavily because the previous coaches were pretty much 'three downs and punt' and 'run the line and punt,'" Elliott said.

"On the first play from scrimmage in Hayden's first game, he split the ends and took all the backs and split them out as flankers. There was nobody in the backfield except the quarterback. He had the quarterback throw the ball on a short pass, and the crowd stood up and cheered because of the fact it was going to be a wide-open situation.

"Those were the things Hayden did. He was adjustable. He could meet every situation the way it was."

Flare and Charisma

As an Iowa quarterback in the 1980s, Chuck Long became the school's career passing and total offense leader.

He completed 782 of 1,203 passes for 10,461 yards and 74 touchdowns from 1982-1985.

Long said it was Coach Hayden Fry who "put the Iowa program on the map. He came into a place that hadn't won in a long time, and had great confidence, a great system and an excellent staff.

"That's what makes an excellent coach—who you hire. He had that flare and charisma about him that told you he was going to be a winner."

Long said he had good feelings about Fry going back to when he was recruited.

"I felt, 'Gosh, there's something about this guy that makes you feel good about yourself,'" Long said. "I remember going into my freshman year and Coach Fry coming into a team meeting room.

"He had already been there two seasons and had losing records in both of them, but you felt he was going to turn it around from day one because of his mannerisms."

That was prior to the 1981 season, which was Long's first on the Iowa campus. "That team wound up going to the Rose Bowl," Long said.

CHUCK LONG

Brooks Calls Fry "Amazing"

An amazing man.

That's what Bob Brooks of Cedar Rapids, Iowa, who broadcast Iowa football games for more than a half-century, called Hayden Fry, who coached the Hawkeyes for 20 years.

"Iowa was desperate for a coach when Fry came here," Brooks said.

"Hayden turned out to be a Hall of Fame coach and certainly will be regarded as one of Iowa's all-time greats. He did it in an era when, in my view, it was harder to get the job done than when Forest Evashevski coached Iowa.

"The rules were much more restrictive, the paperwork had increased, the NCAA was keeping track of recruiting and illegalities. You had to toe the line. Hayden went in as a salesman, and so did his assistants."

Tough Start, Strong Finish

A key member of Hayden Fry's coaching staff at Iowa, and a holdover from the Bob Commings era, was Dan McCarney.

"Dan was so impressive when I interviewed him and hired him off the previous staff," Fry recalled. "It was like he was my son."

McCarney knew all about the lean years as a player at Iowa and later saw what it was like to work for a winner as a coach.

He had lettered as a Hawkeye offensive lineman in 1972, 1973 and 1974 and coached the offensive line under Commings in 1977 and 1978. None of those teams had a winning record.

However, Fry moved him to a defensive line coach in 1979, and defense is where he made his mark until taking over the whole picture when he was named Iowa State's head coach prior to the 1995 season.

McCarney was on the staff when Fry took Iowa to eight consecutive bowl games, then moved to Wisconsin as the defensive coordinator in 1990.

McCarney was a native of Iowa City and a frequent visitor to Iowa games when he was young.

"I came to a few games when Forest Evashevski was the coach, but I saw many more when Jerry Burns and Ray Nagel were doing the coaching," McCarney said.

No. 1 Plays No. 2

Hayden Fry's best team at Iowa was his 1985 squad, which won its first seven games, was ranked No. 1 nationally for five weeks and finished with a 10-2 record and rankings of No. 9 and No. 10 after a 45-28 loss to UCLA in the Rose Bowl.

A classic game that season came on October 19 at Kinnick Stadium when the top-ranked Hawkeyes played No. 2 Michigan.

I covered that game, and excitement throughout the state was at a fever pitch all week.

"It had a Hollywood ending," said Chuck Long, who was Iowa's quarterback.

"The electricity running through the stadium during that game was unbelievable," said Dan McCarney, who then was an assistant on Fry's staff.

Sophomore Rob Houghtlin, who had come to Iowa without a football scholarship, kicked the winning 29-yard field goal as time expired.

"A lot of times, when you have a game of that magnitude, the game doesn't live up to the pregame billing," McCarney said. "But that game against Michigan was one that went beyond it.

"I've been a part of some big bowl victories, but that No. 1 vs. No. 2 matchup in Iowa City is something I'll never forget. Looking at Houghtlin when Michigan called timeout to 'ice' him, he had that unbelievably confident look—almost an arrogance—in his eyes when he came to the sideline.

"It was like he was saying to Michigan coach Bo Schembechler, 'You can call 15 timeouts, Bo, but this thing is going through the uprights.'"

Iowa trailed 10-9 late in the game, but a brilliant play by linebacker Larry Station gave the Hawkeyes hope. Station threw Michigan's Jamie Morris for a two-yard loss on a third-and-two situation that forced the Wolverines to punt.

"We called a stunt," McCarney explained. "But it was Station being Station. He stopped Morris in his tracks and kept Michigan from running out the clock."

Long said Iowa "felt good about that last drive. We had a lot of confidence and a lot of senior leadership. We felt we'd get it done. How could we let the crowd down that day?

LARRY STATION

"We had a little luck going, too. I remember throwing a pass down the sideline that one of their defensive backs dropped late in the game. Of course, we felt we had a touchdown earlier that got called back."

Those Pink Locker Room Walls

Whenever the subject of Bo Schembechler and his Michigan team comes up, former Iowa coach Hayden Fry thinks about the pink walls in the visitors' locker room at Kinnick Stadium.

It was Fry's idea to have the walls painted pink, and the color has evidently freaked out more than one coach, including Schembechler.

"Being a psychology major in college, I discovered that pink is a color that's supposed to calm people down," Fry said. "Maybe even put them to sleep.

"It takes a smart coach to figure out what pink is for, and Schembechler was smart. He, his staff and the student managers went downtown before they played us, bought butcher's paper, and spent all day taping it over the locker room walls."

Another pregame trick Fry said he once used on Schembechler was to switch his guards and center in the warmups.

"I was watching out of the corner of my eye when the guards snapped the ball over the punter's head," Fry said.

"Bo finally said, 'Fry, you're not gonna let that guy snap the ball during the game, are you?'

"I didn't look at him," Fry said. "I had my arms crossed and said, 'Coach Schembechler, we don't plan on punting tonight.'"

Bob Stoops Makes Big Impression

One of the outstanding players in the Hayden Fry era at Iowa was Bob Stoops, who since has gone on to head coaching brilliance at Oklahoma.

Stoops was actually recruited out of Youngstown, Ohio, by Bob Commings in 1978, but later became an All-Big Ten defensive back under Fry.

"I always feel grateful to Coach Commings for giving me the chance," Stoops said. "Once that happened, Coach Bill Brashier [then the Hawkeyes' defensive coordinator] and Coach Fry gave me the chance to play the following season and things worked out."

Stoops made a huge impression early in Iowa's secondary.

"We were playing Purdue in Iowa City in my freshman season," he explained. I had a pretty good collision with a guy over the middle. They were throwing an end route or a post route to him. I had a pretty good line on it, and thought I could get to the ball. But it turned out I couldn't.

"At the end, I sort of zeroed in on him and it didn't work out for either one of us. I think the Purdue player—whose name I don't remember—broke his jaw in a couple of places. I was knocked out on my feet and fell over.

"It ended up that I was only knocked out for a while. Ed Crowley, our trainer, came out and brought me back to the sideline. I actually recovered within a couple of series and later got an interception in the game."

Harty Was "Relentless"

John Harty was never on a winning team in his years at Iowa from 1977-1980, but there was no question about how well he could play football.

"He was relentless," said Dan McCarney, who coached the defensive tackle when he was an Iowa assistant coach.

"John Harty would hurt you as the game went on. I'm not talking illegally, but physically he'd wear you out.

"He spent less time in the weight room than any guy I'd been around, but his strength and power and tenacity were unbelievable. A lot of it was natural. He was one of the best defensive linemen to play college football."

McCarney said Harty was similar to Mark Bortz, another defensive tackle who lettered at Iowa from 1979-1982.

"Harty and Bortz were two of the toughest guys to play the game," McCarney said. "In the last few snaps of the fourth quarter they played as tough and as hard and were as effective as in the first few snaps of the game. It never mattered how tired they got.

"If you were walking down a dark alley, Harty and Bortz were the first two guys you'd grab to go with you."

McCarney recalled a game Harty played against Minnesota in his senior season.

"He had a bad ankle, and there was no question Minnesota wanted to get him out of the game early," McCarney explained. "They were going after his ankle, and somebody gave him a cheap shot from the side.

"On a punt return in his last play of the game, he could hardly walk. Somebody cheap-shotted him again and he limped down the field. The play had just about ended when John came in and hit a guy, who didn't see it coming. John ended up knocking the guy about 15 feet.

"He wasn't going to let those guys get the last shot."

Here's What We're Doing, Charlie

One of the nail-biters in Iowa's 1985 season that produced a 10-2 record was the game against Michigan State.

With the Hawkeyes trailing 31-28 and less than a minute remaining, they had the ball on Michigan State's two-yard line.

The winning play was "quite a story," Iowa quarterback Chuck Long told me years after the Hawkeyes won 35-31.

"We had called a timeout and had none left," Long recalled. "We didn't have a lot of time on the clock. If something didn't work and we got caught in-bounds, we'd have a tough time getting off another play.

"I remember going to the sideline after the timeout and Hayden said, 'Look, Charlie, you're going to call a running play right up the gut, right up the middle, and you're going to fake it and you're going to keep it around the end.'

"He looked at me, as he always did, with great confidence. I said, 'What if I don't get out of bounds?' He said, 'Charlie, you don't need to run out of bounds. You're going to run into the end zone and score.'"

Long said Iowa hadn't run the play before and had worked on it only a few times in practice.

Coaches Noticed Stoops Early

In speaking of Bob Stoops, Hayden Fry told me, "I always knew he was going to be a great one."

Fry and his staff had just come to Iowa in 1979 when word started circulating about Stoops's abilities.

"We were told about certain players," Fry explained. "But I didn't know anything about Bobby. Then, after the first tackling drill, defensive coordinator Bill Brashier said to me, 'I don't know what that kid's name is, but he's the toughest kid on the field.'

"It turned out his father, uncle and brother were coaches. So it was easy to see that he was going to be great."

Stoops was a standout defensive back for Fry's teams from 1979-1982, and his brothers, Mark and Mike, also played for the Hawkeyes.

Hayden Fry's Influence

Chuck Long said the influence of Coach Hayden Fry extended beyond the football field.

"Imagine how much money he raised in the years he was at Iowa," the former Iowa quarterback said. "It had to be the $100 million range. And the pride he put in the state. I remember in the 1980s, when the farmers were having a hard time. They looked forward to Iowa football and we were winning.

"We put a lot of smiles on their faces, and they still talk about it today. When you're building it one brick at a time, you get a lot of satisfaction out of it."

Hawkeyes Played Well at Oklahoma

Iowa's first non-conference game under Hayden Fry wasn't exactly against a patsy.

The game was at Oklahoma, and most people figured the Sooners would be able to name the score.

But Iowa didn't roll over. Oklahoma eventually won 21-6 in the second game of the 1979 season, and Bob Stoops said the Hawkeyes "fought them to the end."

Iowa trailed by a point after three quarters, but Oklahoma put the game away with two late touchdowns.

Stoops, a free safety as a freshman and sophomore and a strong safety as a junior and senior, said Iowa "actually contained [1978 Heisman Trophy winner] Billy Sims. He ended up getting his 100 yards, but he was working for it. That was a hard-fought game.

"In those early games, Coach Fry instilled a great deal of confidence in us. You could feel it coming together for us."

Actually, Iowa's players were feeling pretty good about themselves immediately after the Oklahoma game because they had played so well.

A comment Fry made after the game got everyone's attention. He said if he saw any player smiling, he'd punch him in the mouth.

Some people didn't figure out the message the coach was trying to send to his players and Hawkeye fans. Fry wasn't into abusing his players. He just didn't want them to feel good because of a strong effort. No moral victories for Hayden.

Chuck Long Played Five Seasons

Although Chuck Long—Iowa's career passing leader—lettered from 1982-1985, he was actually on the team for five seasons.

"When I was a freshman in 1981, there was a rule in the Big Ten that you couldn't redshirt freshmen," Long explained to me. "So the coaches had a philosophy that, if you couldn't redshirt players in that first year, let 'em play and then redshirt them in their sophomore year.

"I got a couple of snaps during the 1981 regular season, then played briefly in the Rose Bowl. Then, in my second year, they decided that the rule wasn't good and got rid of it. So then coaches could redshirt freshmen again.

"Some of my classmates got redshirted as sophomores as a result of that. I didn't. I earned a starting job, so the NCAA in my senior year came back and said, 'Hey, we screwed you out of a year.' They said I could have an extra year, so I actually was a senior twice."

As a result, Long wound up going to five bowl games—the Rose Bowl with his 1981 and 1985 teams; the Peach Bowl in 1982, the Gator Bowl in 1983 and the Freedom Bowl in 1984.

"It was good that the NCAA did that," Long said. "It worked out well to me. I had no desire to go to professional football at that time, and I never looked back on it."

Roby Kept Coaches Guessing

Reggie Roby of Waterloo, Iowa, was a consensus All-America punter for Iowa in 1981.

In that season, Roby's 49.8-yard average broke a 32-year NCAA record for punting in a season. He also occasionally kicked field goals. After lettering at Iowa from 1979-1982, Roby punted in the NFL.

However, Roby kept Hawkeye coaches in suspense before finally making his decision on where he wanted to play.

"Hayden Fry and I were recruiting Reggie," explained Dan McCarney, then a member of Iowa's coaching staff and now the head coach at Iowa State. "We were in Waterloo the night before the signing date, and it was between Iowa and Wisconsin on who was going to get him.

"We knew he was the best punter in high school football, and it came down to midnight. We were sitting on pins and needles. While having a sandwich, I was paged with this message: 'Dan McCarney, would you please come to the front desk.'

"I went out there and answered the phone."

"Coach Mac, this is Reggie," Roby told McCarney.

"How you doing, Reggie?" McCarney said.

"I've got some bad news for you," Roby then said.

McCarney still recalls how he felt when he heard Roby's comment.

"My heart went up to my throat," he said.

But then Roby said, "I'm going to be a Hawkeye."

McCarney's reaction was obvious.

"I started screaming and yelling," McCarney told me. "We knew how important Reggie was. Our 1981 team went to the Rose Bowl with a fantastic defense, an OK offense and the best punter in college football."

The Game Gonder Will Remember

The 1983 Iowa-Minnesota football game is one that Ron Gonder, the longtime and now retired play-by-play radio announcer at WMT in Cedar Rapids, Iowa, will always remember.

Not so much because the Hawkeyes won 61-10. Instead, because of something he said.

"It's probably the funniest thing that ever happened to Mike Reilly and me in our 20 years of working together," Gonder said, referring to his color commentator.

REGGIE ROBY

"Iowa quarterback Chuck Long had gotten injured in the game, and they put in Tom Grogan to replace him," Gonder explained. "When Ronnie Harmon dropped a couple of Grogan's passes, I turned to Reilly and said, 'Mike, Harmon seems to be having trouble hanging onto Grogan's ball.'

"I meant that maybe one guy threw a heavier ball or whatever. So then Reilly started to laugh at what I said. Then I realized what I had said and began to laugh, too. We couldn't get the situation under control. We kept laughing.

"We finally took a break and sent it back to the studio. The guy reading the scores started laughing, too. Looking back, I should have said, 'Harmon is having trouble hanging onto Grogan's *passes.*'"

Wrestling's Dan Gable Impressed Stoops

Like a lot of others who went on to become outstanding coaches, Bob Stoops examined the styles of others who were successful.

"John Wooden, Steve Spurrier, Hayden Fry, Dan Gable—all of them impressed me," Stoops said.

"Whenever anyone asks me about coaches, I immediately bring up Gable," Stoops said. "He was a special athlete and a great coach."

Gable was a tremendous wrestler at Iowa State, then became an outstanding coach at Iowa.

"When I was a young volunteer assistant football coach at Iowa, I'd go into the wrestling room and watch those guys work out," Stoops said. "Sometimes they'd actually get me in there to work out, too.

"I always admired the way Coach Gable motivated his athletes and the way he worked. He was a great example for a coach."

Hawkeyes Gained Weight

Iowa didn't score any points in its first trip to the Rose Bowl when Hayden Fry was the coach, but at least the players didn't go hungry.

"We ate buffet-style," Fry told me more than 20 years after the game. "We weren't smart enough because we hadn't been to any bowl games before. The players gained 11 pounds per man."

The extra weight didn't help. Washington blanked the Hawkeyes 28-0.

The "Woozy" Hartlieb-to-Cook Pass

In my many years of covering Iowa football games, a play fashioned by quarterback Chuck Hartlieb and tight end Marv Cook in a game November 14, 1987 at Ohio State stands out as one of the best I saw.

The Hawkeyes were trailing in the final seconds, and Hartlieb says now that he was "knocked pretty woozy on a blitz" several plays earlier.

"I can't say I was thinking that clearly the rest of the game," Hartlieb said. "We had tried on a couple of snaps to get the ball downfield to Quinn Early or one of the other wide receivers, but we struggled to get them open.

"On fourth down, I went to the sideline beforehand and said, 'Let's try and work Marv's matchup.' What we decided to do was send Marv down the sideline and, hopefully, take advantage of a man-to-man situation. I dropped back and looked down the left side of the field as long as I could so I could shade the deep safeties away from Marv.

"I flipped my feet around, and Marv was running a trail down the sideline. Marv was caught man-to-man with the strong safety. I threw it at his back. It allowed

Marv to kind of come back to the ball and let the strong safety run by him."

Hartlieb said Cook "was the one who made the play. He made a great adjustment to the ball, and his heart and desire let him get to the goal line. He easily could have been stopped on the one- or two-yard line."

Indeed, maybe he was. Hartlieb said Bo Pelini, an Ohio State free safety who played in that game and later was a graduate assistant on the Iowa staff, "swears today that Cook was down on the one-yard line. It could have gone either way."

But it was ruled that Cook made it into the end zone to complete the 28-yard play with six seconds remaining in the game. The play gave Iowa a 29-27 victory.

"It was awfully exciting," Hartlieb said. "For years, Coach Fry had talked about the importance of winning in Columbus. He had won at Michigan and in every other Big Ten stadium, but not the one in Columbus. So to get the win for Coach Fry in that fashion was pretty magical."

"Put It in the Banks"

For Gary Dolphin, it was a nervous time. And the nervousness came before the kickoff.

The man from Dubuque, Iowa, had been an Iowa play-by-play announcer earlier in his radio career, but in 1997 he was preparing to do his first game as the new broadcaster in a new format.

Chuck Hartlieb

Iowa's athletic department had decided to use one announcer—Dolphin—and have his broadcasts sent over a large network. Among the play-by-play announcers Dolphin replaced in the new plan were longtime veterans Jim Zabel of Des Moines and Bob Brooks and Ron Gonder of Cedar Rapids.

"At the time, Zabel, Brooks and Gonder were still part of the broadcasts, but they weren't doing play-by-play," Dolphin explained. "I was getting ready to do my first game—Iowa against Northern Iowa—on September 6, 1997, and I literally had just been handed the microphone by Zabel in time for the kickoff.

"I was totally unprepared for what happened. On the first play from scrimmage, Tavian Banks of Iowa ran over left tackle for a 63-yard touchdown. As he approached the goal line, I can remember blurting out, 'You can put it in the Banks!'"

Dolphin's trademark words when a Hawkeye player scores is, "Touchdown Iowa!" and he remembered to say that, too.

Dean Played Best Against the Best

Pat Dean was an All-Big Ten nose guard on Iowa's 1981 Rose Bowl team, and he was a guy "who never stayed blocked."

So said Dan McCarney, the then-Iowa assistant who coached him on Hayden Fry's team.

"Dean was an unbelievable effort guy," McCarney said. "He had limited athleticism, but was a tremendous college player. And he was at his best when he played against the best."

McCarney is now the head coach at Iowa State and recalled a game Dean played against the Cyclones in 1981 when both were at Iowa.

"We had beaten Nebraska the week before, but stunk it up against Iowa State in the following game," McCarney said. "We were bad. One of the hardest things to do after that game was to watch the tape with my defensive line.

"I got after Pat. He had gone from being brilliant against Nebraska to stinking it up when we lost to Iowa State 23-12.

"But I'll never forget what happened the next week against UCLA. They couldn't block him, we had a great offense, and Dean wound up being named National Player of the Week."

Iowa upset the sixth-ranked Bruins 20-7, and Dean made 10 unassisted tackles.

Rose Bowl Ring, No. 41 Jersey Goes into Casket

Ron Stoops was only 54 years of age when he died. His sons, Bob, Mark and Mike, played for Iowa.

"When my dad died, we folded the No. 41 Iowa jersey and set it next to him in the casket," Bob Stoops said. "We all wore No. 41, and Coach Fry and several of the other coaches brought it to the funeral. I also left my Rose Bowl ring in the casket."

The Tough Tim Dwight

No one played football with any more zest at Iowa than Tim Dwight, a consensus All-America return specialist in 1997.

Dwight was also a standout pass receiver who is Iowa's career leader with 2,271 yards from 1994-1997. Despite those numbers, many Iowa fans felt the skilled player from Iowa City didn't get the ball as often as he should have.

"Dwight's toughness is what stood out, although that might be too bland a description," said Iowa play-by-play radio announcer Gary Dolphin.

"I have never been around a player who enjoyed contact as much with the possible exception of Tom Rusk [a Hawkeye linebacker from 1975-1978].

"To me, Dwight was a linebacker in the body of a kick returner and wide receiver. As great as he was on offense, he always gave you the impression he'd rather be on defense so he could hit somebody."

"Best of My Life as an Athlete"

In 1985, Iowa quarterback Chuck Long not only finished second to Bo Jackson of Auburn in the closest Heisman Trophy vote in history, he won the Maxwell Award that went to the nation's top player and he was the Big Ten's most valuable player.

Long became the first quarterback in NCAA history to pass for more than 10,000 yards—he had 10,461—and was a first-round choice of the Detroit Lions in the 1986 NFL draft.

Tim Dwight

"It never dawned on me that I'd finish second in the Heisman voting," Long said. "If you shoot for those types of goals, it becomes a kind of a selfish deal—like you're there only to win a Heisman Trophy. So I just focused my goals to coincide with our team's goals.

"My years at Iowa were the best of my life as an athlete. You grow so much as a person in college, and I grew a lot under the tutelage of Coach Hayden Fry and offensive coordinator Bill Snyder. They were great guys.

"And the Iowa fans were outstanding and very supportive. I also enjoyed dealing with the media. You guys were very good. And a big thing was being part of Iowa's turnaround. It's fun being part of a turnaround as opposed to going somewhere and keeping it going."

Scary Situation in the Radio Booth

Scary things can sometimes happen in the radio booth.

Ron Gonder of WMT in Cedar Rapids, a longtime Iowa radio play-by-play announcer, told me of a situation during a Hawkeye game at Ohio State.

Gonder said Mike Reilly, his color commentator, had given a pass to the booth to an Iowa fan from Iowa City the night before the game.

"The man was standing in the back of the booth, and our engineer said, 'Be ready in 30 seconds,'" Gonder said. "Suddenly, the man who was Reilly's guest began making noises and clutching his chest.

"Reilly turned around and the guy is saying, 'Mike, help me. I think I'm having a heart attack!' I was on the air. Reilly went back to lay the guy down on the floor in the back of the booth. Then Reilly left the booth to holler for a doctor.

"Four guys in white coats came to help. While this is going on, I'm giving the wrong yard lines and wrong ball carriers. I'm thinking, 'Is this guy going to die in the booth?' And we're making no sense out of the game."

Gonder said the ailing man was placed on a stretcher and taken to a hospital.

"It turned out he had an irregular heartbeat," Gonder said. "They gave him some medication and he flew back to Iowa City after the game."

"Class Act by Eddie"

There was plenty of emotion connected with the September 13, 1997 game when Iowa played Tulsa in Iowa City.

The Hawkeyes won 54-16, but the emotion came when tailback Tavian Banks broke Ed Podolak's single-game rushing record. Podolak's record of 286 yards was set against Northwestern on November 9, 1968.

Podolak was in the broadcast booth—doing his job as radio analyst alongside play-by-play announcer Gary Dolphin—during the 1997 game that saw Banks break his record by rushing for 314 yards against Tulsa.

"What I'll always remember was that it was Podolak who was the first guy to give Banks a standing ovation

TAVIAN BANKS

when he broke the record," Dolphin said. "When Banks ran off the field, Eddie—who is an emotional guy—had tears running out of his eyes.

"None of us like to have our records broken, but there was Eddie with watery eyes and applauding as he stood. I thought it was a real class act by Eddie."

Harmon Loses Four Fumbles in Rose Bowl

Iowa's 1985 team spent five weeks ranked No. 1 nationally, but lost its chance to finish as the best in school history because of a disappointing 45-28 loss to UCLA in the Rose Bowl.

The Hawkeyes wound up No. 9 in the final United Press International poll and No. 10 in the Associated Press poll.

Although Ronnie Harmon caught a career-high 11 passes for 102 yards and also led his team in rushing with 55 yards in the Rose Bowl game, the senior running back lost four fumbles as the Hawkeyes fell behind at halftime 24-10. Harmon had coughed up the ball only once on a fumble in Iowa's 10-1 regular season.

Consequently, his problems in the Rose Bowl were a source of puzzlement.

"It was so uncharacteristic of him," said Dan McCarney, who then was Iowa's defensive line coach and now is the head coach at Iowa State. "It was a shock to all of us on the sideline. Harmon had great ball security, tremendous speed, and his hands were as great as anyone

RONNIE HARMON

I've seen in a collegiate running back. To this day, I can't figure it out."

Many years after the game was played, Iowa quarterback Chuck Long—who completed 29 of 37 passes for 319 yards against UCLA—defended Harmon.

"I know Ronnie, and Ronnie helped us win a lot of games," Long said.

Harmon led Iowa's 1985 team in both rushing with 1,166 yards and pass receiving with 699 yards.

Of the Rose Bowl loss, Long said, "We turned the ball over a lot, but UCLA played well. They had a talented team, even though their record didn't show it as much as ours did. They had a lot of future NFL draft picks. We had our chances, but didn't capitalize on them."

Harmon was named to a couple of first-team All-America squads and was a first-team All-Big Ten player.

The Harmon Look-Alikes

Iowa running back Ronnie Harmon and his younger brother, teammate Kevin Harmon, looked so much alike that people sometimes had difficulty telling one from the other when they didn't see their uniform numbers.

Reporters were even confused after Iowa's 1985 team lost to UCLA 45-28 in the Rose Bowl.

"That was the game in which Ronnie lost four fumbles," said Ron Gonder, who then was the play-by-play radio announcer for WMT in Cedar Rapids, Iowa. "After the game, some Los Angeles media guys were waiting with Iowa reporters, including me, in the interview area.

"'Do you know what Ronnie looks like?'" they asked us. "When we said yes, they asked if they could hang around until Ronnie came out. So out comes Kevin Harmon. We all went over to him, thinking it was Ronnie.

"When the first question started out, 'Ronnie…,' Kevin interrupted with, 'Kevin! Kevin! Kevin!'

"The L.A. guys kind of melted away. Everybody else kind of withdrew."

Fry's Final Season

The 1998 season, which turned out to be Hayden Fry's last as Iowa's coach, was not pretty.

The Hawkeyes' 15-game winning streak over Iowa State ended with a 27-9 loss in the second game, and the 3-8 season—which turned out to be the worst in Fry's years at Iowa—continued to go downhill.

The Hawkeyes lost their final five games, with heated rival Minnesota as the team that saddled Fry with a 49-7 defeat in his final game as a coach. His record with the Hawkeyes was 143-89-6 and his record at Iowa, North Texas State and Southern Methodist was a combined 232-178-10 in 37 seasons. His teams made 17 bowl appearances.

Buildings Named After Fry

Hayden Fry told me his wife, Shirley, said to him, "You might be the only guy on the Iowa campus to have two buildings named after you—the Hayden Fry Football Complex and the J. Hayden Fry Center for Prostate Cancer Research."

Then Fry paused.

"As I look back at it, you can't buy things like that," he said. "It's great that people are honoring me for whatever reason. But I don't suggest that anyone get prostate cancer to get a building named after him."

Before being diagnosed with prostate cancer, Fry said he had "been healthy for 47 years. I never missed a practice, never missed a game. I never realized how valuable health is because I had never been sick.

"I was a dumb old football coach. I thought you had to be at work at 5:30 in the morning and go home at midnight. I didn't have a physical exam for 20 years."

Chapter 5
Odds and Ends

$5 a Game for Future President

Not many play-by-play radio announcers of collegiate football games go on to become president of the United States.

But that was the case with Ronald Reagan, who worked for Iowa stations WOC in Davenport and WHO in Des Moines as a young man.

George F. Davison Jr., a Des Moines attorney and a Sunday newscaster on WHO, said Reagan was hired by WOC in the fall of 1932 to broadcast several Iowa football games from Iowa City. The Minnesota game was among them.

"The pay was $5 a game, plus round-trip bus fare from Davenport," Reagan said in April 1974, while speaking at the 50th anniversary of WHO.

Davison said Reagan joined WOC as a staff announcer on February 10, 1933.

"At the time, WOC and WHO were both owned and operated by the Palmer family," Davison explained. "In May 1933, the WOC studios in Davenport were closed. Reagan and other WOC employees moved to Des Moines and the WHO facilities. WOC returned to the air in late-1934 as a separate facility."

After his radio days, Reagan took a screen test in Hollywood in 1937, acted in 53 films and later went into politics. He was elected this nation's 40th president in 1980, and served two terms.

Reichardt One of the Best

One of the best players to wear an Iowa uniform— yet a guy who never played for a team that had a winning record in his years as a Hawkeye—was fullback Bill Reichardt, who lettered in 1949, 1950 and 1951.

Reichardt was named the Big Ten's most valuable player in 1951 even though his team didn't win a conference game.

"I maybe should be in the Guinness Book of World Records," Reichardt told me while reflecting on his career. "I may be the only athlete in intercollegiate sports, male or female, who was named the most valuable player on a team that didn't win a conference game."

Iowa's only victories in a 2-5-2 season in 1952 were over Kansas State and Pittsburgh. The Hawkeyes tied Minnesota and Notre Dame. They lost Big Ten games to Purdue, Michigan, Ohio State, Illinois and Wisconsin.

Reichardt rushed for 737 yards as a senior, and still ranks 12th on Iowa's career rushing list with 1,665 yards in three seasons.

Iowa's "Highest Illegally Paid Player"

More than a half-century after Bill Reichardt was a star fullback for Iowa, he claims he was the "highest illegally paid player in the history of Iowa football."

Reichardt explained that he got that distinction after deciding to play for the Hawkeyes instead of Southern California.

"My mom wanted me to get out of Iowa City," he said.

"I accepted a scholarship to Southern California and was already on the train that was headed there. But just before the train pulled out of town, my dad, Iowa coach Eddie Anderson and Dr. Red Scanlan got on board to talk to me."

Reichardt said Anderson "had never asked me to go to Iowa—he just assumed I'd go there." But people interested in convincing Reichardt he should be a Hawkeye swung into action once they knew Reichardt was on the train bound for California.

"Dr. Scanlan was head of an Iowa booster club and was our family doctor," Reichardt said. "He said, 'Here's what we can do for you,' and offered me $200 a month for four years—a lot of money in those days—plus a job when I got out of school. I was to pick up the $200 in cash at his office on the first of every month.

BILL REICHARDT

"Anderson didn't hear what Dr. Scanlan told me about the money, but I got off the train and decided to attend Iowa. While I was in school, my room, board, books and tuition were paid, and so were my fraternity dues."

Why Reichardt Has a Limp Today

One of Bill Reichardt's teammates at Iowa was Lou Ginsberg, a guard on teams in 1945, 1948, 1949 and 1950.

"Louie died a few years ago," Reichardt said. "But just before he died, I called him on a Saturday afternoon. I'd heard he was in the hospital, dying of cancer. I said to him, 'Louie, how are you doing?' He said, 'Why would you think of me?'

"I said, 'Louie, I'll bet I've thought of you once a day for the last 45 years.' Louie said, 'Why would you do such a thing?'

"I said, 'Louie, you were in front of me on every play I ran at Iowa, and you never threw one [bleeping] block, and that's why I walk with a limp now.'

"Louie laughed and laughed and laughed. He died three or four days later."

Coach Defines His Pissants

Bob Commings, who had been a lineman for Iowa in the 1950s, returned to coach the Hawkeyes from 1974-1978.

The story is told of a speech he gave in Des Moines early in his years as the coach. He kept referring to some of his players as "pissants."

When it got to the question-and-answer part of the program, a man in the audience stood. The man cleared his voice and said, "Coach Commings, I'm somewhat confused by your continuous referral to a pissant. Can you define pissant for us?"

"A pissant is a guy who can't block or tackle," Commings explained.

The Gary Snook Story, and How it Grew

In the 1960s, Iowa had a quarterback named Gary Snook, who was known for his exploits off the field as well as on the field.

Stories made the rounds often about how Snook was a party boy who often consumed more cold drinks than his body could handle. Friends of Coach Jerry Burns say he likely knew the risk he was taking when he recruited Snook.

Burns and others consistently heard tales of how Snook was drunk either inside or outside some Iowa City establishment. When Burns would learn of the latest story concerning his quarterback, he'd go to the source and say, "Where did you get that information?"

The guy might say, "The dry cleaner told my wife."

Then Burns would go to the dry cleaner, who told him he'd heard the story from someone else. After a while,

Coach Bob Commings

the coach would reach a dead end in his quest for knowledge.

So no one knows for sure how many of the stories involving Snook, who lettered in 1963, 1964 and 1965, were true

Indeed, a few days after one particular game in which Snook played, Burns supposedly heard that his quarterback had been seen drunk on a street in Iowa City the night before the game.

However, one of Burns's assistant coaches had made bed-check at midnight at the motel in a town well beyond Iowa City where the coaches and players stayed the night before games.

Snook and his roommate were both in their beds.

Afterward, Burns told a friend he seriously doubted that Snook could have gotten out of bed, sneaked out of his room, then out of the motel, obtained a car, then driven to Iowa City to get drunk well after midnight.

Reichardt's First Game

Bill Reichardt, the Iowa fullback who became the Big Ten's most valuable player in 1951, had an emotional start to his Hawkeye career.

His first season was 1949 and Iowa's first opponent was UCLA—Eddie Anderson's final year as the Hawkeyes' coach.

"My fraternity roommate was George Constantine of Fort Dodge, who was one of the most delightful guys I ever knew in my life," Reichardt said. "On the Friday night before the UCLA game, he went home to Fort Dodge to get some stuff for our room and was killed in an automobile crash.

"I was horribly devastated. I went down to St. Mary's Church and sat there all night lighting candles. Eddie Anderson was a devout Catholic who went to church nearly every day. At 6 a.m. Saturday, he walked into the church and saw me praying.

"He thought I was praying for the game. I was so excited to be on the team, but I was exhausted before the game. In the locker room, Anderson said in front of the whole squad, 'Carideo [assistant coach Frank Carideo], who are you going to put in there at fullback?' Carideo said, 'We're going to put in [Gerald] Nordman.'

"'Carideo, don't you know Nordman can't remember the plays?' Anderson said.

"'OK, we'll put [Donald] Riley in there,' Carideo said.

"'Carideo, what are you trying to do, ruin me?' Anderson asked.

"'Well, we'll put that Reichardt in there,' Carideo said.

"'OK, Reichardt, you're in there,' Anderson said."

Reichardt said he then went to team physician Shorty Paul and said, "Shorty, I don't have my knee taped. I don't have my ankles taped."

Reichardt said Paul "tugged on Anderson's sleeve and said, 'Dr. Anderson, Reichardt doesn't have his knee taped.'"

Anderson then said, "You tell Reichardt to put a Band-Aid on his knee."

Not an Easy Sell

Dan McCarney lettered as an Iowa offensive lineman from 1972-1974 and captained the team as a senior.

But there was no certainty that McCarney, even though he grew up in Iowa City, would play football for the Hawkeyes.

"There was definitely some doubt that I'd go to Iowa," McCarney explained. "Johnny Majors was coaching Iowa State at the time, and Iowa's program was really down. Majors and Jackie Sherrill, who then was Iowa State's defensive coordinator, were recruiting me.

"I wasn't anything special as a player, but they wanted me because I was from Iowa City. I knew they wanted somebody out of Iowa City. Majors and Sherrill were outstanding recruiters, and I signed a conference letter of intent with Iowa State. I signed it a week or two before the national signing date."

Enter Mike Cilek.

"Mike had been an Iowa quarterback," McCarney said. "I had lunch with him and we talked a long, long time about what it meant to grow up in Iowa City. That had as much to do with my decision to go to Iowa as anything. It worked out fine for me, but we didn't win many games, didn't win any championships and didn't go to any bowl games."

McCarney said the recruiting style of Majors, who was Iowa State's head coach from 1968-1972, and Sherrill, who was on the Cyclones' staff in those seasons, stayed with him.

OZZIE SIMMONS

"I've incorporated a lot of their recruiting and fol-low-up philosophies into how I recruit now," McCarney said.

Ozzie and Ossie

Ozzie Simmons, a first-team All-Big Ten player for Iowa in 1934 and 1935, and his brother, Don, found an interesting way to get to Iowa City from their home in Fort Worth, Texas.

"They hopped a freight train and came all the way up here that way," explained George Wine, who is re-tired after spending 25 years as Iowa's sports information director.

"Finding a place to play for black guys was tough in those days. But an Iowa alumnus encouraged the Simmons brothers to go to Iowa."

Ozzie lettered in 1934, 1935 and 1936 as a half-back. Don lettered in 1935 and 1936 as an end. Ossie Solem was the Hawkeyes' coach.

"Ossie gave Ozzie and Don a workout, they did pretty good and wound up staying," Wine said.

"Ain't They Blocking for You?"

One of Iowa's most embarrassing losses came in 1950, when Ohio State lowered the boom on the Hawkeyes 83-21 at Columbus.

"We knew Vic Janowicz of Ohio State won the Heisman Trophy that day," Iowa fullback Bill Reichardt said of a Buckeye player who ran for two touchdowns, passed for four and set a Big Ten record with 10 extra points. "We fell behind 28-0 very quickly, and there was a strong wind coming out of the south. We couldn't pass or kick.

"I had to run kickoff after kickoff back because Ohio State was scoring so many touchdowns. Late in the game, one guy from Ohio State nailed me on a play. It ticked me off. They had my arms pinned back, and a guy from Ohio State used his fist to smack me.

"He said, 'What's the matter, Reichy? Ain't they blocking for you?'"

The Trip to Havana

A week after the 62-point loss at Ohio State in 1950, Iowa pulled off a 13-0 victory over Minnesota and later tied Notre Dame 14-14 before closing the season with a 14-6 loss at Miami, Florida.

"When we got to Miami, the black guys on the team were picked up in two convertibles and the Jewish guys were also driven off separately," said fullback Bill Reichardt. "None of them could stay in the hotels with the rest of us."

"How did that make the rest of you feel?" I asked Reichardt.

"We didn't know any better," he answered. "They went off in Cadillac convertibles and we got picked up in a school bus. We thought they had a better deal."

Reichardt said a journey to Cuba was also part of that road trip.

"The coaches and players flew to Havana after the game," he explained.

"I was the first player off the bus, and we went to a girlie show. What horrible poverty there was down there. Fathers were pimping for their daughters, and it was the most depressing experience of my life up to that point.

"Shorty Paul, the team doctor, gave everybody a penicillin shot on the way home—whether they needed it or not."

That Lonely Feeling After a Game

Jerry Burns, who was Iowa's coach from 1961-1965, seemed to have a soft spot in his heart for quarterback Gary Snook, who passed for 3,738 yards and 20 touchdowns as a Hawkeye.

That was good enough to get him chosen in the fourth round of the 1966 NFL draft by St. Louis.

However, Burns told friends he always felt badly that, after a home loss, no one was there to greet Snook when he came out of the locker room. Other players had numerous members of their families to say some encouraging words in those tough years.

COACH JERRY BURNS

Key to the Elks Club Door

One season when Forest Evashevski was the coach, Iowa's players and coaches stayed at a hotel in Detroit the night before their game at Michigan in Ann Arbor.

One of Jerry Burns's friends tells the story that several of the assistant coaches wanted something cold to drink, so Burns—then one of the staff members—suggested they go to the Elks Club. Another assistant said, "Hey, Jerry, at most Elks Clubs you've got to be a member to be admitted."

As the story goes, Burns said, "Don't worry about it. They think I'm Jesus Christ at that place, and we'll have no trouble getting in."

When the Iowans got to the Elks Club, a man in charge peered through the front door, recognized Burns and said, "Well, Jesus Christ!"

Putdown Artists Reichardt and Duncan

Bill Reichardt and Randy Duncan, both star former Iowa players from Des Moines, still enjoy needling one another long after their football careers ended.

Although he was a consensus All-America quarterback in 1958, Duncan was not named to Iowa's all-time team by Gannett News Service in 2000. Chuck Long was chosen the quarterback. However, Reichardt was chosen the fullback.

"If there'd have been a second team—which there wasn't—Duncan might have made it," Reichardt said while laughing at the putdown of his friend.

Reichardt formerly owned a clothing store, stressing that he sold quality suits.

"I always used to say I have a suit that was eight years old," he said. "People would ask me what I'd do with the suits once that got to be that age. I'd say, 'I take the shoulders in as much as I can, I let the [bottom] out all that I can, then I give 'em to Randy Duncan.'"

When Reichardt made an unsuccessful attempt to run for governor in Iowa in 1992, he claims Duncan said, "Reichardt belongs in an insane asylum."

Said Duncan: "Don't believe anything Reichardt says. What I really said was that Reichardt needs a frontal lobotomy. As for football, I've talked to other players who said Reichardt never practiced, and that he could have been twice as good as he was."

Jones's Mythical National Champions

His name was Howard Jones, and he put a major imprint on Iowa football history.

Jones, a Yale graduate who was known as a strong disciplinarian, was hired as the Hawkeyes' coach prior to the 1916 season.

His teams wound up winning mythical national championships in 1921 and 1922. Both teams had 7-0 records. Jones's Hawkeyes had a 20-game winning streak, still the longest in Iowa football history.

The streak included the last three games of a 5-2-0 season in 1920, the seven games in both 1921 and 1922 and the first three games of the 1923 season. In all, Jones had a 42-17-1 record from 1916-1923.

After his success at Iowa, Jones went on to establish an outstanding program at Southern California.

Included in the 1921 season was a 10-7 victory over Notre Dame, then coached by the immortal Knute Rockne. The Fighting Irish brought a 20-game winning streak into the game and were heavily favored.

But Iowa got the jump on Notre Dame, scoring all of its points in the first quarter on Gordon Locke's short fourth-down touchdown run and a 38-yard field goal drop-kicked by Aubrey Devine.

Notre Dame's captain and right end was a man whose name would loom large in Iowa's football future.

He was Eddie Anderson, a native of Mason City, Iowa, who coached the Hawkeyes' 1939 team that acquired the nickname "Ironmen" and featured the legendary Nile Kinnick, who won the Heisman Trophy.

Iowa's First Two All-Americans

Lester Belding, an end from Mason City, Iowa, became the Hawkeyes' first consensus All-American as a sophomore in 1919.

Belding was a three-time All-Big Ten selection. He was one of the nation's standout pass receivers in his era. He also starred in track, and captained the team in 1921.

However, the first Hawkeye to make an All-America team was Fred Becker of Waterloo, Iowa, a tackle who earned the honor in 1916.

LESTER BELDING

And Finally...

The experience of researching and writing *Tales from the Iowa Sidelines* has given me the privilege of experiencing a Hawkeye football highlights film in print.

From a modest beginning in 1889—when Iowa fielded its first football team, had no coach and played a one-game schedule—no one could have imagined that Nile Kinnick would come out of tiny Adel, Iowa, and win a Heisman Trophy in 1939 while being coached by a medical doctor, or that Kirk Ferentz would coach a team in 2002 that won all eight of its games in the Big Ten.

Those are things of which dreams are made. Heading into the 2003 season, Iowa teams have played 1,039 games. The Hawkeyes have won 520, lost 480 and tied 39.

I've been around for only a small fraction of those games. But I've seen enough of them to be able to safely predict that football will be alive and well for many more years at a place where the legend of Nile Kinnick lives on.

Celebrate the Heroes of College Athletics
in These Other 2003 Releases from Sports Publishing!

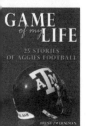
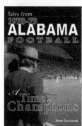